RR
—
BTG

W9-BZO-677

ROB RAINFORD'S
BORN TO GRILL

OVER 100 RECIPES
FROM MY BACKYARD TO YOURS

PHOTOGRAPHY BY MIKE McCOLL · FOREWORD BY RITA DeMONTIS

appetite
by RANDOM HOUSE

COPYRIGHT © 2012 Rob Rainford

All rights reserved. The use of any part of this publication, reproduced, transmitted in any form or by any means electronic, mechanical, photocopying, recording or otherwise, or stored in a retrieval system without the prior written consent of the publisher—or in the case of photocopying or other reprographic copying, license from the Canadian Copyright Licensing Agency—is an infringement of the copyright law.

Appetite by Random House and colophon are trademarks

Library and Archives of Canada Cataloguing in Publication is available upon request

ISBN: 978-0-449-01563-6

Cover and interior photos: Photos with Sauce by Mike McColl www.photoswithsauce.ca
The recipe for Jack-a-Rita on page 96 courtesy of Greg Cosway, founder of Toronto's Festival of Beer

Printed and bound in the USA

Published in Canada by Appetite by Random House,
a division of Random House of Canada Limited

www.randomhouse.ca

10 9 8 7 6 5 4 3 2

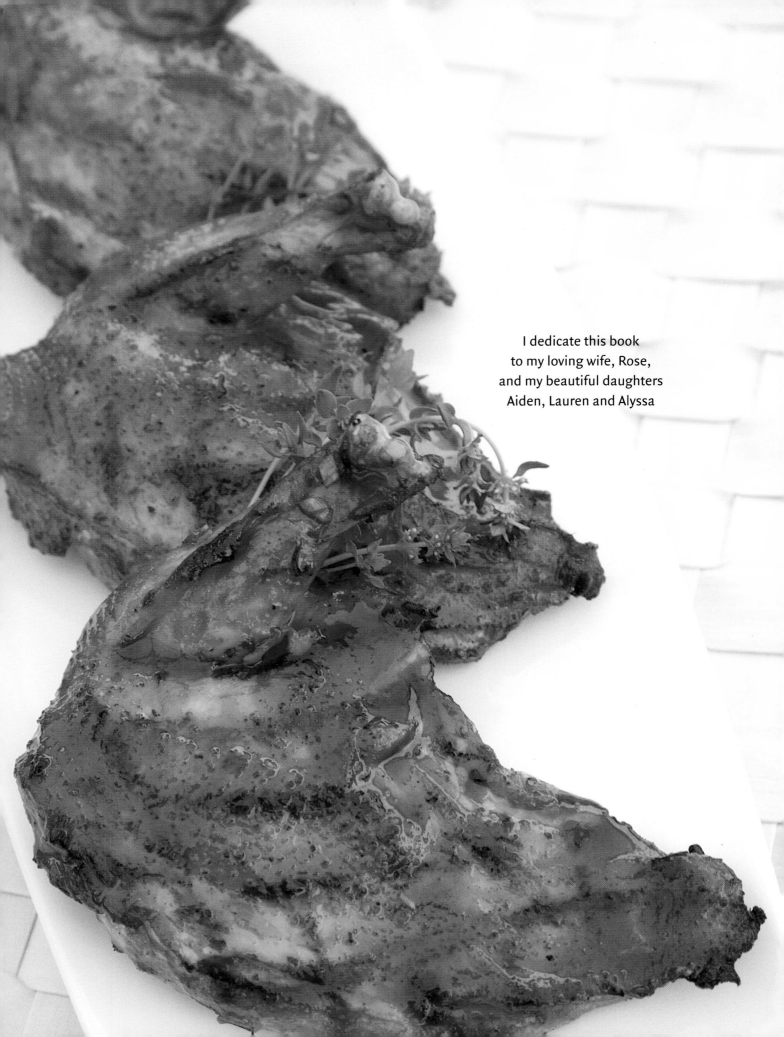

I dedicate this book
to my loving wife, Rose,
and my beautiful daughters
Aiden, Lauren and Alyssa

CONTENTS

FOREWORD

I FIRST MET ROBERT back in the late 1990s, at a student competition at George Brown culinary college in Toronto. We had both been invited to judge the event and, with hundreds of students and staff milling about and the general frantic pace of the competition, it was a little overwhelming to say the least.

But Robert, a tall and elegant man, was confidence personified, a cool presence tinged with what I perceived was a wicked sense of humor with a side of deadpan thrown in for good measure. He seamlessly moved among the students who were competing, speaking to each of them and minutely examining plate after plate with those big brown eyes of his, digging a spoon here, a fork there, until he was finally satisfied with the end results. We all were.

At that moment it struck me that Robert was a man of principle, a little on the strict side and with an unabashed dedication to his work that was inspiring to perceive.

I liked him right away, especially when he talked about his family, sharing the Italian side of his life, including anecdotes about tomato-preserving with his mother-in-law. I shrieked with laughter, telling him I had failed miserably at this sacred rite of my heritage, and we both giggled at the memories. His face would literally light up with brilliant flashes of warmth and it was obvious how much joy his family life brought him.

Of course, knowing Robert's work through his television career and various Toronto food events only added to the sense of camaraderie I shared with him that day in the kitchens of George Brown College.

Throughout the years our work kept us bumping into each other, either at food shows or industry events. And it's like that old saying about good friends: you may not meet up often, but when you do connect, it's like you just saw each other the day before.

One day, at yet another food event, I watched Robert up close and personal as he participated in a black box competition surrounded by the tools of his trade, including his beloved grill. It was a cool day so the warmth of the grills kept us close to the action. At the height of the competition, I observed something come over Robert, his eyes darting from food item to food item, obviously formulating a plan of action with the ingredients he had at hand.

It was fascinating to watch how he tuned out the world, his long fingers delicately dancing over the various plates, coaxing layer upon layer of flavors from the items in his black box. It might have been a treasure chest, so intent was he in finding the tasty jewels within.

Nothing fazed him—not the clock, not the crowds—and he completed his task with barely a ripple of tension. Just that smile of satisfaction indicated that his meal was complete. My stars, his finished plate tasted awesome! He won, of course, and a new-found respect for the great grill master was born.

With Robert, it's apparent he demands the best not only of those around him, but mostly of himself. It shows in the way he handles food, how he communicates with those around him, and how strong his dedication and love is to what he holds so dear.

I've watched Robert create some of the grandest dishes to come off a grill, and I've shared the most humble of meals as well. That he applies the same strict discipline to both is a given and, to me, the sign of a brilliant man.

For Robert, it's all in the pleasure his food brings, in his recipes that are detailed yet easy to follow, something I'm sure you will find in this book. He's inviting you to his table with a tome rich in delicious discoveries. It certainly is a feast for all your senses.

Rita DeMontis, National Food Editor, Toronto Sun | SUN Media

INTRODUCTION

I'M ROB RAINFORD and I was Born to Grill. Some of you may know me from my work on Food Network Canada's *Licence to Grill*, others from my previous grilling books. Either way, you're going to love this cookbook.

Born to Grill is the next stop on my grilling odyssey. I've had the opportunity to travel and cook in some interesting places. Sure, I've cooked for celebrities, but entertaining my family and friends is what really inspires me. This book contains 20 menu suggestions that will wow your guests. I've assembled my favorite recipes for this book and I know that if you follow The Rainford Method—my way of deconstructing a recipe so that anyone can make it successfully—you'll produce some great meals. I've grilled every recipe in my own backyard, and had an awesome time doing it.

My lifelong love affair with grilling can be traced back to the sights and smells emanating from barbecues my family had when I was a child. Having been born in Jamaica, I come from a culture that uses the grill extensively. Our national dish might be ackee and saltfish but what most ex-pats and tourists remember about Jamaica is the jerk chicken and pork cooking on wide-open charcoal grills. The love of food and cooking runs deep in my family and I was fortunate enough to inherit my grandmother's famous jerk chicken recipe.

I grew up in downtown Toronto in a colorful neighbourhood, surrounded by the aromas of barbecues cooking up native foods from different cultures. When my older brother, Howard, started cooking, he propelled family meals to a new level in our house and he spruced up some favorite dishes that my mom had been making for years. Howard cooked most of our family meals when I was growing up with my brothers Richard and Alvin, and my sister, Marcia. That period in my life really shaped my love for food.

After a lot of soul searching and many talks with my family I decided to learn to cook from the ground up so, in the 1990s when I was already in my mid-20s, I enrolled in George Brown College's culinary school. Attending George Brown was the best decision I could have made. The college gave me the skills to cook professionally in a competitive environment. I was taught by some of Canada's best instructors, such as chef Allen Brown who took a special interest in me. He made me feel as if it wasn't too late to learn how to be a chef, and that there were professional chefs in my corner.

Being good at grilling is not necessarily innate but it can be learned and appreciated over time. I have a passion for life, so my grill is just an extension of that philosophy. What makes the grill so unique is that, because you're outdoors, you feel as if you're communing with nature while you're preparing a meal. So, get out in the fresh air and grill up some great food for your family and friends.

GRiLLiNG THE RAiNFORD WAY

WHAT I DO WHEN I prepare a meal—the methodology of how I hold my chef's knife and how I light my grill—can be summed up by this: I listen to my instincts! And of course you should too—whether you're a seasoned pro or new to barbecuing. Sure, you can follow my instructions and my recipes step by step, but what's really important is that you listen to your instincts. That's how you end up with a great dish.

Another important part of the Rainford Method is understanding fire. The more you barbecue, the more you'll gain knowledge about how fire affects food.

HOW TO START A CHARCOAL GRILL

I use both gas grills and charcoal grills, but I have to say that these days I'm *really* into charcoal. I love the whole process, from getting the barbecue started to cooking food inches away from burning coal.

The first thing to take into consideration is the *kind* of charcoal. I recommend hardwood (i.e., lump) charcoal, of which there are many types—try experimenting and you'll be amazed at the subtle differences. There's even a Hawaiian lump charcoal that I find quite nice.

You'll need one layer of coals for direct grilling and two layers for indirect grilling. I use a Looftlighter charcoal lighter (see page xv). It's a great gadget; the coals are ready in no time. Just point it at the charcoal, press the button, and they will ignite. Another easy and reliable method is to use a chimney starter, which most barbecue stores should have. Fill the top with charcoal, then place scrunched-up newspaper in the bottom. Place on the grill grate and use a long wooden match to light the newspaper. The coals will burn and start to develop a thick white ash in about 20 to 30 minutes. Turn out the coals into the grill and reposition the grate.

If you are creating a two-zone fire for indirect grilling, spread the charcoal evenly over half of the bottom of the grill. If you are building a fire for direct grilling, it's still a good idea to leave at least a small space where there are no charcoals so that you have an "out."

Make sure the charcoal is well lit—covered in white ash—before you start cooking. And make sure the grate is nice and hot.

DIRECT OR INDIRECT GRILLING?

Grilling food over *direct* heat is quick and easy. It's perfect for burgers, thin steaks and pieces of chicken or fish, and also for vegetables and kebabs.

Indirect heat is the way to go for everything else. It's best for larger and/or tougher cuts of meat that require one to three hours of slow, gentle cooking: think of ribs, a whole chicken, a leg of lamb—all succulent, tender, juicy. I also use indirect grilling when I want to create a nice sear on a piece of meat before cooking it over even heat. (This also works for delicate items that could benefit from char marks *and* gentle cooking.)

DIRECT GRILLING

For direct grilling, I have a clear idea of the perfect temperature. Technically, it's 400°F (200°C), which you could call medium-high, but which I call the *Five-Steamboat Rule*. Hold your hand a few inches above the grill grate and quickly count "one steamboat, two steamboats, three steamboats . . ." If you can't get to five steamboats, your grill is too hot!

With gas grills, make sure you preheat the barbecue for at least 15 minutes before you check the heat. For a charcoal grill, the coals should be bright orange and covered with a light layer of ash.

INDIRECT GRILLING—OR HOW TO BUILD A TWO-ZONE FIRE

With a two-zone fire, you have a hot zone and a cool zone. A one-zone fire (in a charcoal grill this means the coals are arranged evenly over the bottom of the grill) is the reason why most people end up burning their food when grilling larger cuts.

For a charcoal grill, spread the charcoal evenly over *half* of the bottom of the grill. Keep an eye on the thermometer until it's the correct temperature (as directed in the recipe). For a gas grill, preheat the barbecue for about 15 minutes, then adjust one side or section to the desired heat and turn off the other side completely. This will be the indirect heat area. Keep the lid covered during the cooking time.

USING A DRIP PAN: When you are indirectly grilling a large cut of meat that contains a lot of fat, using a drip pan or tray is a real lifesaver—you don't want the fat to drip down, flare up and create the wrong kind of smoke. I use disposable baking pans made of foil. Place the pan underneath the grates where your cool zone will be. Fill the pan three-quarters full with water—to which you may add some of your favorite beer, wine or spirit for a really great aromatic steaming effect!

USING WOOD CHIPS: Wood chips are great for adding a smoky flavor. I use a combination of wet (soaked) and dry wood chips. (An entire packet of wet chips would burn too slowly, and a packet of dry chips would burst into flames.) If you are using a foil pouch instead of a smoker box, poke holes all over it—the more holes, the more smoke.

Lay the packet on the hot side of the grill. Wait until you see smoke enveloping the cabin. When you're ready to barbecue, be prepared to work quickly. You don't want the lid off the barbecue for too long.

RAINFORD BARBECUE TIPS

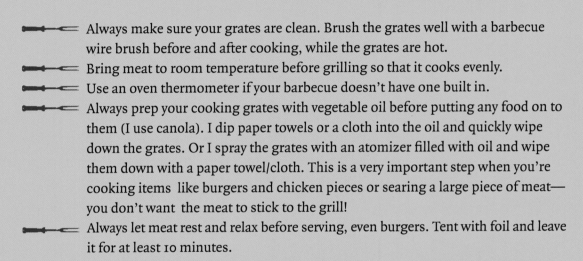 Always make sure your grates are clean. Brush the grates well with a barbecue wire brush before and after cooking, while the grates are hot.

Bring meat to room temperature before grilling so that it cooks evenly.

Use an oven thermometer if your barbecue doesn't have one built in.

Always prep your cooking grates with vegetable oil before putting any food on to them (I use canola). I dip paper towels or a cloth into the oil and quickly wipe down the grates. Or I spray the grates with an atomizer filled with oil and wipe them down with a paper towel/cloth. This is a very important step when you're cooking items like burgers and chicken pieces or searing a large piece of meat— you don't want the meat to stick to the grill!

Always let meat rest and relax before serving, even burgers. Tent with foil and leave it for at least 10 minutes.

A NOTE ON THE RECIPES

Most of the recipes in this book are for eight people, but of course you can halve or double the recipes, depending on how many guests you're grilling for. And feel free to make the portion sizes smaller—for example, a 6 oz (180g) instead of 8 oz (250 g) piece of fish.

If you see an ingredient in a recipe that you don't like, don't be afraid to make substitutions. Also, you don't have to cook the complete menu all at once; my recipes are designed to be mixed and matched. You should adapt my recipes and make them your own!

TRICKS OF THE TRADE

KEY RAINFORD BARBECUE TOOLS

BARBECUE TONGS
Long barbecue tongs give good distance between you and the grill.

WIRE BRUSH
A wire brush will help you keep the grill free of debris. It's important to keep your grill clean at all times.

SYRINGE (FLAVOR INJECTOR)
A kitchen syringe will allow you to place flavors directly into the meat or chicken you're cooking. Just think about your favorite flavors being more pronounced in every bite.

SMOKER BOX OR FOIL POUCHES
The wood flavor in your food will give that barbecue taste you've come to expect. Try different types of wood like elder, pear, maple, mesquite or hickory. You can buy them in different sizes from chips to chunks. The size of wood depends on the length of the grilling process.

STAINLESS STEEL GRIDDLE
This is a great accessory to add to your barbecue, because it adds the element of a flat top. Just think about the pancakes, bacon and eggs you'll be able to cook!

THE LOOFTLIGHTER CHARCOAL LIGHTER
This tool was designed by a friend of mine from Sweden, Richard Looft. It's a hand-held device that gets your coals glowing in minutes. The lighter doesn't shoot flames, but heats a blown air stream to 1250°F (676°C). It heats coals in 20 minutes, and is available in most barbecue stores.

MEAT THERMOMETER
These 3-second reading thermometers are widely available. The readings are accurate to approximately 0.7°F, and they usually have a water-resistant design.

RAINFORD'S STAPLE RECIPES

CHICKEN STOCK

The most economical way to buy chicken parts is to buy a whole chicken and dismantle it yourself. Keep the rest of the carcass and store it in a resealable plastic bag in the freezer until you have three, then make this from-scratch stock.

3 chicken carcasses, about 1 lb (500 g) each
8 cups (2 L) cold water
1 onion, coarsely chopped
1 rib celery, coarsely chopped
½ large carrot, coarsely chopped
8 parsley stems
3 sprigs of fresh thyme
2 bay leaves
½ tsp (2 mL) whole black peppercorns

THE RAINFORD METHOD

1. Break apart chicken carcasses and put in a large stock pot. If you can't find chicken carcasses, you can also buy 3 lb (1.5 kg) of chicken bones.
2. Add cold water to the bones, and bring to a boil. Once boiling, skim the surface with a spoon until all the visible fat is gone.
3. Add onion, celery, carrot, parsley, thyme, bay leaves and peppercorns to the pot.
4. Simmer for 1 hour and strain.

Makes 6 cups (1.5 L)

 Tip: Don't sweat it if you don't have the time or inclination to make my chicken stock. All the recipes in the book will work just fine with stock from the store.

JERK MARINADE

¾ cup (185 mL) white vinegar
½ cup (125 mL) orange juice
¼ cup (60 mL) olive oil
¼ cup (60 mL) soy sauce
1 lime, juiced
2 Tbsp (30 mL) garlic powder
1 Tbsp (15 mL) dried thyme leaves
1 Tbsp (15 mL) ground allspice
1 ½ tsp (7.5 mL) dried red chili flakes
1 ½ tsp (7.5 mL) dried ground sage
1 ½ tsp (7.5 mL) freshly ground
      black pepper
1 tsp (5 mL) kosher salt
¾ tsp (4 mL) ground cinnamon
¾ tsp (4 mL) ground nutmeg
1 cup (250 mL) chopped onion
3 green onions, finely chopped
1 Scotch bonnet chili, seeded and chopped

THE RAINFORD METHOD

Blend all ingredients together in a food
processor until smooth.

Makes 1 ¾ cups (450 mL)

RAINFORD'S BARBECUE SAUCE

¾ cups (185 mL) apple juice
½ cups (125 mL) ketchup
3 Tbsp (45 mL) cider vinegar
2 tsp (10 mL) soy sauce
1 tsp (5 mL) Worcestershire sauce
1 tsp (5 mL) molasses
½ tsp (2 mL) chili powder
½ tsp (2 mL) garlic powder
¼ tsp (1 mL) freshly ground black pepper

THE RAINFORD METHOD

Combine the apple juice, ketchup, vinegar,
soy sauce, Worcestershire sauce, molasses,
chili powder, garlic and pepper in a small
saucepan set over medium heat. Simmer for
20 minutes or until thickened, then remove
from heat.

Makes 1 cup or 250 mL

*Feel free to double or triple the ingredients in this
sauce, depending on how much you need.*

RAiNFORD'S GRiLLiNG TEMPERATURE CHART

BEEF STEAKS
Rare	125–130°F	52–54°C
Medium-Rare	130–140°F	54–60°C
Medium	140–150°F	60–65°C
Medium-Well	155–165°F	68–74°C

BONE-IN BEEF ROASTS
Rare	125–130°F	52–54°C
Medium-Rare	130–140°F	54–60°C
Medium	140–150°F	60–65°C
Medium-Well	155–165°F	68–74°C

BONELESS, ROLLED BEEF ROASTS*
Rare	not recommended	
Medium-Rare	not recommended	
Medium	not recommended	
Medium-Well	not recommended	
Well done	170°F	76°C

* For boneless, rolled beef roasts, an internal temperature of 170°F (76°C) is recommended because surface bacteria may have been rolled into the center of the roast.

RACK OF LAMB
Rare	125–130°F	52–54°C
Medium-Rare	130–140°F	54–60°C
Medium	140–150°F	60–65°C
Medium-Well	155–165°F	68–74°C

LAMB CHOPS
Rare	125–130°F	52–54°C
Medium-Rare	130–140°F	54–60°C
Medium	140–150°F	60–65°C
Medium-Well	155–165°F	68–74°C

PORK CHOPS
Rare	not recommended	
Medium-Rare	not recommended	
Medium	not recommended	
Medium-Well	155–165°F	68–74°C
Well Done	175–185°F	80–85°C

VEAL RACKS
Rare	125–130°F	52–54°C
Medium-Rare	130–140°F	54–60°C
Medium	140–150°F	60–65°C
Medium-Well	155–165°F	68–74°C

VEAL CHOPS
Rare	125–130°F	52–54°C
Medium-Rare	130–140°F	54–60°C
Medium	140–150°F	60–65°C
Medium-Well	155–165°F	68–74°C

WHOLE CHICKEN	170–175°F	76–80°C
CHICKEN PIECES	170–175°F	76–80°C
WHOLE TURKEY	170–180°F	76–82°C
BURGERS	160°F	71°C

RAiNFORD FiSH GRiLLiNG TiPS

WHOLE FISH, FISH FILLETS AND STEAKS
Fish is done when the flesh flakes easily with a fork. Also look for an opaque appearance all the way through. If you're unsure, an internal temperature of 155°F (68°C) is recommended.

SHRIMP AND LOBSTER TAILS
Flesh is fully cooked when it turns opaque and firm. Be careful to avoid overcooking shrimp or lobster.

THIS FIRST MENU was pulled together over a few beers with my really good friend chef Samir Hanna. We were sitting on my back deck and I was telling him that I'd like to start my book with a tribute to him.

Samir has helped me immensely in my kitchen life. I thought back to all the meals we cooked together at one of the restaurants we worked at. The dishes we had to prepare for the customers had none of the ethnic flare of the meals Samir and I would cook for each other and for our staff.

Now that I've started this journey of cooking and grilling my way, I am determined to begin this cookbook with the kind of food Samir and I both love.

A TASTE OF NORTH AFRICA

Egyptian **LAMB KOFTAS**

Cinnamon-Scented **TOMATO-JASMINE RICE**

FRESH TOMATO SALAD with Grilled Red Onion

TAHINI SAUCE with Lemon

Yogurt-Garlic **CUCUMBER DIP**

EGYPTiAN LAMB KOFTAS

Koftas are like North-African-spiced mini burgers on skewers. They're very delicate, so be sure to sear them well before turning to prevent them from sticking to the grate.

¾ lb (375 g) ground lamb
¼ lb (125 g) ground beef
1 large onion, finely grated
¼ cup (60 mL) finely chopped fresh parsley
1 egg
1 Tbsp (15 mL) extra virgin olive oil
2 cloves garlic, finely grated
1 Tbsp (15 mL) ground allspice
1 ½ tsp (7.5 mL) kosher salt
2 tsp (10 mL) freshly cracked black pepper
Canola oil for greasing

THE RAINFORD METHOD

1. Mix all the ingredients together in a large bowl until well combined.
2. Place mixture in a resealable plastic bag and refrigerate for 24 hours.
3. Take the mixture out of the bag and form into eight even-size portions, shaped like mini footballs (as in American football, not soccer). Run a skewer widthwise through each kofta.
4. Preheat the grill to medium-high (if you are using charcoal, heat the coals until a thick white ash develops). Oil the grate with canola oil.
5. Place the koftas on the hot grill. Make sure to sear them well before you try to turn them, and turn carefully or they will break apart.
6. Grill the koftas until a meat thermometer registers an internal temperature of 150 to 160°F (65 to 71°C).
7. Remove from skewers and serve in pita bread.

Makes 8 servings

CiNNAMON-SCENTED TOMATO-JASMiNE RiCE

One of the chefs I worked with in Asia showed me a great trick that I call "the old knuckle test." Add the rice to a rice cooker, then place your middle finger on top of the rice and pour in enough liquid to come to the first joint of your finger. Works every time.

1 ½ cups (375 mL) jasmine rice

1 cup (250 mL) tomato passata

¾ cup (185 mL) water

1 tsp (5 mL) kosher salt

1 cinnamon stick

2 plum tomatoes (fresh or canned), seeded and diced

THE RAINFORD METHOD

1. Rinse the rice under cold running water, moving the rice around with your fingers. Continue rinsing until the water runs clear with no white milkiness. Drain the rice well.
2. Place the rice in the rice cooker and add tomato passata, water, salt and cinnamon stick.
3. Cook according to the instructions and, when the button pops, remove the lid and fluff the rice. Fluffing the rice simply means using a dinner fork to loosen all the grains of rice. Remove the cinnamon stick and fold in the chopped tomatoes.

Makes 6 servings

Tip: I like to use a rice cooker. It just makes it a lot easier as it takes the small chance of messing up out of the equation: when the button pops it's done. A rice cooker steams the rice, so no peeking. If you don't have a rice cooker, please use your favorite traditional method.

FRESH TOMATO SALAD
with GRiLLED RED ONiON

I had some leftover Champagne (as you do) so I added it to the vinaigrette and it was fabulous.
If you have no bubbly lying around, Champagne or white wine vinegar are good too. For best flavor,
chop the tarragon at the last minute.

1 red onion, sliced into 1-inch (2.5 cm) rings
6 plum tomatoes
2 Tbsp (30 mL) canola oil
Kosher salt and freshly cracked
       black pepper to taste

Vinaigrette
¼ cup (60 mL) olive oil
¼ cup (60 mL) cider vinegar
¼ cup (60 mL) Champagne
3 Tbsp (45 mL) finely chopped fresh tarragon
1 tsp (5 mL) Dijon mustard
Kosher salt and freshly ground
       white pepper to taste

THE RAINFORD METHOD

1. Two hours before grilling, whisk the vinaigrette ingredients together in a bowl and add onion rings, tossing to coat. Marinate at room temperature.
2. Fire up your charcoal or preheat your gas grill. Grilling temp should be around 325 to 350°F (160 to 180°C). Prep the grill for cooking over direct heat.
3. Core the tomatoes then cut them lengthwise into quarters. You want large, chunky pieces for this rustic grilled salad.
4. Remove the onion rings from the vinaigrette, reserving the vinaigrette. Brush the onion rings lightly with a little canola oil and season them with salt and black pepper.
5. Place the onion rings on the grill and cook until lightly charred, 6 to 10 minutes per side on medium-high heat.
6. Remove onion rings from the grill and set aside to cool slightly. Whisk the vinaigrette until nice and thick.
7. To assemble the salad, combine the tomatoes, cooled onion rings and vinaigrette in a bowl and you're done.

Makes 6 to 8 servings

Tip: *Canola oil has a higher smoke point than say, olive oil, so brushing the onion rings with canola before grilling them will prevent the onions burning. Serve this salad buffet-style or in individual salad bowls.*

TAHINI SAUCE with LEMON

Buy your favorite brand of tahini for this flavorful sauce. Any leftovers will keep in the fridge for about 1 week.

¼ cup (60 mL) vegetable stock
½ cup (125 mL) tahini
2 cloves garlic, finely grated
1 Tbsp (15 mL) red wine vinegar
2 tsp (10 mL) fresh lemon juice
1 tsp (5 mL) ground cumin
½ tsp (2 mL) kosher salt
Freshly ground black pepper to taste

THE RAINFORD METHOD

1. Stir the vegetable stock into the tahini to thin it out.
2. Stir in the garlic, vinegar, lemon juice, cumin, salt and pepper until blended.
3. Cover and refrigerate until ready to serve.

Makes 4 to 6 servings

YOGURT-GARLIC CUCUMBER DIP

1 ¼ cups (310 mL) seeded and finely diced English cucumber
1 tsp (5 mL) kosher salt
2 cups (500 mL) whole-milk yogurt
2 Tbsp (30 mL) finely chopped fresh mint
1 Tbsp (15 mL) olive oil
1 Tbsp (15 mL) fresh lemon juice
2 cloves garlic, finely grated
¼ tsp (1 mL) freshly ground black pepper

THE RAINFORD METHOD

1. Place the diced cucumber in a colander and sprinkle with ¾ tsp (4 mL) salt. Toss very well and let drain in the sink for 30 minutes.
2. While the cucumber drains, spoon the yogurt into another colander lined with a coffee filter and let stand for 15 minutes.
3. When cucumber has drained for 30 minutes, grab a few layers of paper towel, place the cucumber in the middle of the layers and press down lightly to draw out as much excess moisture as possible from the cucumber.
4. In a bowl, stir together the strained yogurt, cucumber, mint, olive oil, lemon juice, garlic, pepper and remaining salt.
5. Cover and refrigerate until ready to serve.

Makes 4 to 6 servings

ON ONE OF MY FIRST days at culinary school, I met a fellow student who helped me get my first paying job in the 90s at a Middle Eastern restaurant. Some of the staples in the restaurant kitchen were lamb, couscous and zucchini.

On one of the slower nights I was inspired to play in the kitchen and this menu was the result. Putting this menu together when I was writing the book sent me down memory lane and reminded me of leaving school and heading to that restaurant all those years ago.

MORE FLAVORS FROM AFRICA

2

Grilled **LEG OF LAMB**

Grilled **MIDDLE-EASTERN PATTIES**

Stuffed **ZUCCHINI BOATS**

Herbed **COUSCOUS WITH TOMATOES** and **PINE NUTS**

LEMON-LOVE MARTINI

GRiLLED LEG OF LAMB

This one's for my friend George Karamitos the Greek Golfer. I serve the lamb with stuffed zucchini and couscous but it also pairs well with a fresh tomato salad or rice; the options are endless, really!

⅔ cup (160 mL) Greek or other white wine
⅓ cup (80 mL) Greek or extra virgin olive oil
1 onion, cut into quarters
8 cloves garlic, coarsely chopped
2 Tbsp (30 mL) coarsely chopped fresh rosemary
9 lb (4 kg) leg of lamb
Canola oil for greasing

THE RAINFORD METHOD

1. Place wine, olive oil, onion, garlic and rosemary in a blender and blend until puréed.
2. Place lamb leg in a large roasting pan and rub all over with the wine mixture. Cover and marinate in the fridge for 24 hours.
3. Bring leg of lamb up to room temp about 1 hour before grilling.
4. Fire up your charcoal grill and prep the grill for cooking over indirect heat. You need a medium-high temperature of around 350°F (180°C) to grill the leg of lamb. For gas grills, preheat the grill to medium-high then turn off one burner to achieve indirect heat. For best results, place a drip tray underneath the leg of lamb *(see Tip)*.
5. Once the grill is hot, scrape all the marinade off the leg of lamb. Oil the grate with canola oil.
6. Sear the lamb on direct heat first, until it is a dark brown color on all sides. Move the lamb leg to the cooler part of the grill and close the lid. Be sure not to peek too much because opening the lid will cause the temperature to drop.
7. For medium-rare, grill for about 15 to 20 minutes per pound (500 g), until a meat thermometer registers an internal temperature of 130 to 140°F (54 to 60°C). Remove the lamb from the grill and let it rest for about 20 minutes before carving.

Makes 8 to 10 servings

Tip: *Be sure to use a drip tray set directly under the lamb when it's on the cooler side of the grill. This will ensure all drippings from the lamb don't mess up the barbecue. You can even add a little Greek white wine and water to the drip tray to add a little steam.*

GRILLED MIDDLE-EASTERN PATTIES

Beef, chicken or turkey all work well in these tasty patties so use whatever ground meat you prefer.

2 lb (1 kg) ground beef, chicken or turkey

6 Tbsp (90 mL) finely chopped fresh cilantro

4 Tbsp (60 mL) grated onion

2 jalapeño or serrano chilies, seeded and diced

4 cloves garlic, finely grated

1 tsp (5 mL) ground coriander

1 tsp (5 mL) ground cumin

1 tsp (5 mL) ground cinnamon

1 tsp (5 mL) ground allspice

1 tsp (5 mL) freshly ground black pepper

Kosher salt to taste

Canola oil for greasing

24 slider buns

THE RAINFORD METHOD

1. Combine whatever ground meat you choose with cilantro, onion, chilies, garlic, coriander, cumin, cinnamon, allspice, black pepper and salt.
2. Make a tiny patty and grill it off so you can taste it to ensure the flavor and seasonings are to your liking. It's good? That's great.
3. Make 24 even-size mini round patties and place them in the fridge for about 30 minutes to firm up.
4. Fire up your charcoal grill and prep the grill for cooking over indirect heat. You need a medium-high temperature of around 350°F (180°C) to grill the patties. For gas grills, preheat the grill to medium-high then turn off one burner to achieve indirect heat. Oil the grate with canola oil.
5. Grill your patties for 3 to 4 minutes on each side on direct heat. Then move them to the indirect side for an additional 5 to 6 minutes.
6. When the patties are done, remove them to a clean plate and allow to rest. While the patties are resting place the buns on the grill to warm, then assemble the sliders—they're great served with homemade mayo (recipe on page 58)—and enjoy.

Makes 8 servings

STUFFED ZUCCHINI BOATS

8 green zucchini
8 slices grilled bacon (*see Tip*)
1 cup (250 mL) small cubes aged white cheddar
2 plum tomatoes, seeded and diced
2 Tbsp (30 mL) diced onion
1 clove garlic, finely grated
1 ½ tsp (7.5 mL) finely chopped fresh basil
Kosher salt and freshly ground black pepper to taste

THE RAINFORD METHOD

1. Wash and trim zucchini, then cut each one into 3-inch (8 cm) lengths (the size of a shot glass). Scoop out seeds with a small melon baller. Be careful not to cut completely through the skins.
2. Fire up your charcoal grill and prep the grill for cooking over indirect heat. You need a medium-high temperature of around 350°F (180°C) to grill the zucchini. For gas grills, preheat the grill to medium-high then turn off one burner to achieve indirect heat.
3. Chop the grilled bacon and mix with the cheddar, tomatoes, onion, garlic, basil and salt and pepper in a bowl.
4. Fill each zucchini boat with the bacon mixture and place on a rimmed baking sheet. Pour a little water onto the baking sheet to create steam. Place the baking sheet on the cooler side of the grill and close the lid.
5. Grill for 20 to 30 minutes, until zucchini boats are tender.

Makes 8 servings

 Tip: *To grill the bacon, place the slices on a rimmed baking sheet and place it on the grill heated to a medium-high temperature of about 350°F (180°C).*

HERBED COUSCOUS
with TOMATOES and PiNE NUTS

1 ½ cups (375 mL) couscous
2 ¼ cups (560 mL) boiling water
½ tsp (2 mL) kosher salt
¼ cup (60 mL) extra virgin olive oil
¼ cup (60 mL) fresh lemon juice
1 Tbsp (15 mL) finely grated lemon zest
3 cloves garlic, grated or pushed through a garlic press
1 tsp (5 mL) ground cumin
2 cups (500 mL) peeled, seeded and diced beefsteak tomatoes
1 ½ cups (375 mL) diced red onion
¼ cup (60 mL) lightly toasted pine nuts
¼ cup (60 mL) golden raisins
2 Tbsp (30 mL) finely chopped fresh parsley
2 Tbsp (30 mL) finely chopped fresh mint
Kosher salt and freshly ground black pepper to taste

THE RAINFORD METHOD

1. Put couscous in a large bowl. Pour the boiling water over it, add the salt and give it a stir. Cover with plastic wrap and let stand for 10 to 15 minutes until couscous is swollen and tender.
2. In a small bowl, combine olive oil, lemon juice, lemon zest, garlic and cumin, give it a good whisk and set aside.
3. Fluff the couscous with a fork and add the tomatoes, red onion, pine nuts, raisins, parsley and mint. Pour over the vinaigrette and give it a good toss. Season with pepper and more salt. Let sit at room temperature for a least 1 hour before serving.

Makes 6 to 8 servings

Tip: *To peel fresh tomatoes, core them then cut a small cross with a sharp knife at the opposite end. Put them in a large pot with 3 quarts (3 L) boiling water for about 20 to 30 seconds. Remove them from the boiling water then plunge them in ice water to stop the cooking. Now you can peel them easily. To remove all the seeds, halve the tomatoes lengthwise and give them a gentle squeeze.*

LEMON-LOVE MARTiNi

My friend and manager Greg Cosway, who has an extensive background in bartending, provided me with this complimentary martini drink to serve with my lamb dish. This martini is a great version of a timeless classic and the lemon flavors work really well with the lamb in this menu!

Ice
6 oz lemon vodka
5 oz Triple Sec or Cointreau
3 to 4 oz fresh lemon juice
  (from 2 or 3 lemons)
1 lemon
½ cup (125 mL) rock sugar
  (granulated sugar will also work)
4 lemon twists

1. Fill a cocktail shaker two-thirds full with ice. Add the lemon vodka, Triple Sec and lemon juice to taste. Shake vigorously.
2. Cut the lemon into wedges and use the wedges to wet the edges of 4 chilled martini glasses.
3. Spread the sugar out on a plate and dip the wet rims of the glasses in the sugar.
4. Strain the cocktail into the glasses. Garnish each with a lemon twist, pour the leftover ice from the shaker into each glass and serve immediately.

Makes 4 large martinis

THIS MENU REFLECTS my love both of beef and using charcoal in my cooking. I like to try as many new things as I can so, when I sat down to assemble my thoughts, I decided to shrink all these dishes down so everyone can have a taste of everything when it's passed around. I know red meat is not for everyone but do try out this menu. Prime rib, beef kabobs and flank steaks are just the tip of the iceberg when it comes to beef and, when followed with the chocolate fondue, this menu brings home a little taste of my Jamaican roots.

FOR THE LOVE OF BEEF

③

Rotisserie **HERB PRIME RIB**

Spice-rubbed **RIB-EYE KABOBS** *with* **SALSA VERDE**

Thai-style Barbecued **FLANK STEAK** *with* **ASIAN NOODLE SALAD**

Italian **CUCUMBER AND TOMATO SALAD**

JAMAICAN CHOCOLATE FONDUE

ROTISSERIE HERB PRIME RIB

For maximum flavor allow the prime rib to sit in the thyme rub overnight, but don't apply the salt until just before you start to cook it.

6 Tbsp (90 mL) finely chopped fresh thyme

10 cloves garlic, pushed through a garlic press

2 Tbsp (30 mL) finely chopped fresh rosemary

2 Tbsp (30 mL) finely chopped fresh oregano

Freshly cracked black pepper to taste

7 to 10 lb (3.15 to 4.5 kg) bone-in prime rib roast

¼ cup (60 mL) grapeseed oil (or just enough to coat the prime rib)

Kosher salt to taste

THE RAINFORD METHOD

1. Stir together the thyme, garlic, rosemary, oregano and pepper. Rub the prime rib all over with the oil then coat with the thyme mixture. Refrigerate overnight.

2. Fire up your charcoal or preheat your gas grill and prep the grill for using the rotisserie. Grilling temp should be around 325°F (160°C). For charcoal grilling, you're ready to grill when a thick white ash has appeared on the coals. Move most of the hot coals to the middle of the grill and place a few on either side to create heat in the middle of the grill where the meat will be rotating.

3. Rub the prime rib with salt to taste and load it onto the rotisserie rod, doing your best to center the roast. Finger tighten the rotisserie forks either side of the prime rib (you may have to use a pair of pliers to tighten the forks securely).

4. If you're using a gas grill, place a drip pan directly on the grates in the middle section of the grill. This will help to catch any fats that drip from the prime rib. You can place a little water in the bottom of the drip pan to help create a moist environment if you wish. Just remember you will be cooking with the lid closed for about 1 ½ to 2 hours, depending on how you like your meat.

5. Put the rotisserie rod on the grill, making sure the rod is secure. Close the lid, set the motor speed to low, then let your grill do the rest of the work. A good rule of thumb is to cook the prime rib for 20 minutes per pound (500 g). For medium-rare meat, you will be looking for an internal temperature of 135°F (57°C).

6. Once your prime rib is done to your liking, take it off the rotisserie and let it sit for 10 to 15 minutes before slicing it.

Makes 8 servings

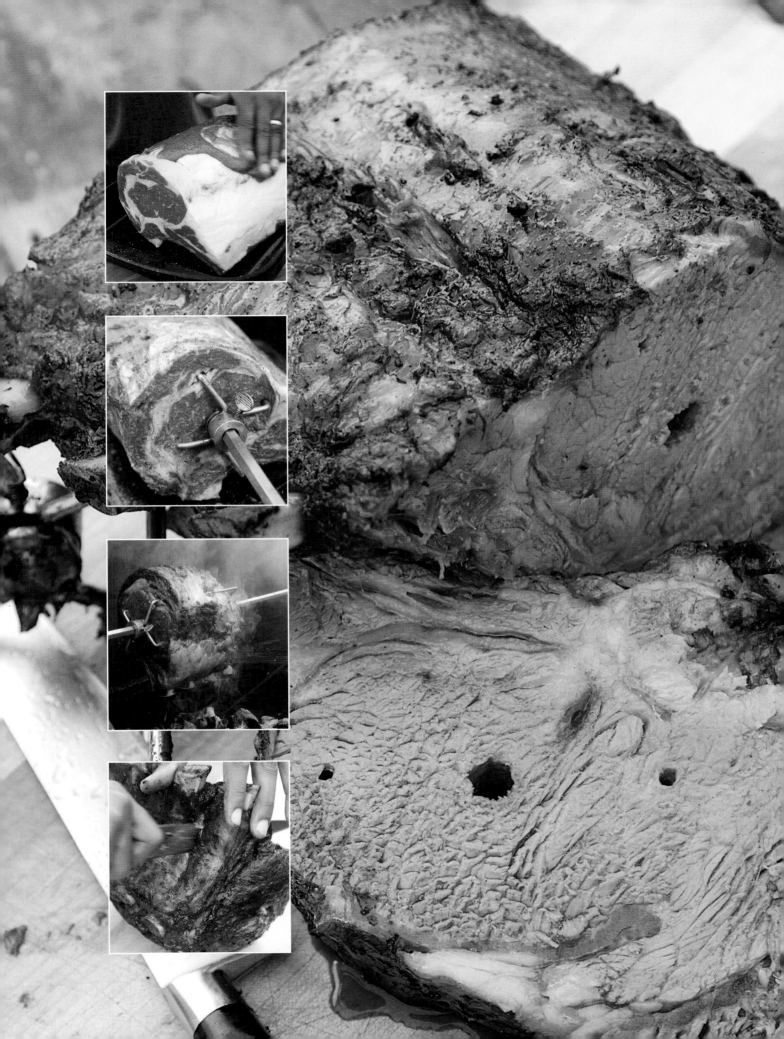

SPICE-RUBBED RIB-EYE KABOBS
with SALSA VERDE

Rub

2 tsp (10 mL) kosher salt

1 tsp (5 mL) packed light brown sugar

½ tsp (2 mL) freshly ground black pepper

½ tsp (2 mL) garlic powder

½ tsp (2 mL) chili powder

Kabobs

4 boneless rib-eye steaks,
      each about 12 oz (375 g) and
      1 to 1 ½ inches (2.5 to 4 cm) thick

Extra virgin olive oil

12 metal skewers, or wooden skewers soaked
      in water for at least 30 minutes

Canola oil for greasing

Salsa Verde

½ cup (125 mL) tightly packed
      fresh basil leaves and tender stems

½ cup (125 mL) tightly packed fesh
      Italian parsley leaves and tender stems

2 anchovy fillets

1 clove garlic, coarsely chopped

6 Tbsp (90 mL) extra virgin olive oil

1 Tbsp (15 mL) red wine vinegar

1 tsp (5 mL) seeded and finely chopped
      jalapeño chili

¼ tsp (1 mL) kosher salt

⅛ tsp (0.5mL) freshly ground black pepper

THE RAINFORD METHOD

1. Mix all the ingredients for the rub in a large bowl.

2. Cut the rib-eye steaks into 1- to 1 ½-inch (2.5 to 4 cm) chunks, removing and discarding any large pieces of fat. Add the chunks of steak to the bowl and toss to coat them evenly with the rub. Add just enough oil to lightly coat the meat and mix well.

3. Thread the chunks onto the skewers, leaving a little room between each chunk. Set aside at room temperature for 20 to 30 minutes before grilling.

4. Fire up your charcoal grill and prep the grill for cooking over indirect heat. You need a medium-high temperature of around 350°F (180°C) to grill the kabobs. For gas grills, preheat the grill to medium-high then turn off one burner to achieve indirect heat.

5. In a food processor, finely chop the basil, parsley, anchovy fillets and garlic. Add the remaining sauce ingredients and let the machine run until the sauce is well combined, 1 to 2 minutes, scraping down the sides of the bowl occasionally.

6. Brush the cooking grate clean and brush with canola oil. Grill the skewers over direct high heat, with the lid closed as much as possible, until cooked to your desired doneness, 4 to 6 minutes for medium rare, turning once or twice and swapping the positions of the skewers for even cooking. Serve warm with the sauce.

Makes 8 servings as part of this menu; 4 to 6 if served alone

THAI-STYLE BARBECUED FLANK STEAK with ASIAN NOODLE SALAD

This Thai-style flank steak is my twist on a flavor profile I have come to love. Living in Toronto, a city with such diverse cultures, inspired this dish.

Steak

½ cup (125 mL) soy sauce

½ cup (125 mL) ketjap manis
    (Indonesian sweet soy sauce)
    or regular soy sauce

⅓ cup (80 mL) fresh lime juice

3 cloves garlic, finely grated

2 green onions, sliced (white parts only;
    reserve green ends for salad)

2 Thai chilies, seeded and finely chopped

2 Tbsp (30 mL) packed brown sugar

2 Tbsp (30 mL) sesame oil

2 Tbsp (30 mL) fish sauce

1 Tbsp (15 mL) finely grated fresh ginger

1 Tbsp (15 mL) finely chopped lemongrass,
    outer stalk removed

1 lb (500 g) flank steak or flat-iron steak

Canola oil for greasing

Kosher salt to taste

Salad

2 oz (60 g) vermicelli-style dry rice noodles

Canola or grapeseed oil

1 head Boston lettuce, washed,
    dried and leaves separated

1 English cucumber, sliced

1 red onion, sliced into rings

2 cups (500 mL) cherry tomatoes

⅓ cup (80 mL) fresh mint leaves, divided

⅓ cup (80 mL) fresh cilantro leaves, divided

⅓ cup (80 mL) fresh basil leaves, divided

⅓ cup (80 mL) dry roasted peanuts, chopped

2 Tbsp (30 mL) sesame seeds

THE RAINFORD METHOD

1. For the steak, combine the soy sauce, ketjap manis, lime juice, garlic, green onions, chilies, sugar, sesame oil, fish sauce, ginger and lemongrass in a bowl until well blended and sugar has dissolved. Remove half the marinade and set aside to use as a dressing. Place the remaining marinade in a resealable plastic bag.

2. Lightly score the beef in a crosshatch (diamond) pattern and place in the bag with the marinade. Give it a massage and place in fridge for 4 hours.

▶

3. Fire up your charcoal or preheat your gas grill. Grilling temp should be around 350°F (180°C). For charcoal grilling, you're ready to grill when a thick white ash has appeared on the coals. Place three-quarters of the hot coals on one side of the grill and place a few on the other side. Oil the grate with canola oil.

4. Remove the beef from marinade, discarding the used marinade. Season the beef generously with salt. Place the beef on the grill and cook for about 5 minutes per side or until well marked and rare, or longer if you prefer your meat less rare. Transfer the beef to a cutting board and let rest for 5 minutes before slicing. Slice very thinly against the grain.

5. Meanwhile, soak the rice noodles in warm water about 20 minutes or until tender. Drain well and drizzle lightly with oil to prevent sticking.

6. Combine the smaller lettuce leaves, cucumber, onion, tomatoes and half of the mint, cilantro and basil in a bowl. Add the reserved unused marinade and toss until well coated.

7. Mound a portion of the noodles in the center of a serving platter and top with the salad. Arrange the beef over the salad and garnish with peanuts, sesame seeds and remaining herbs.

Makes 6 to 8 servings as part of this menu; 4 if served alone

Tip: *If you prefer to serve this on individual plates, line each plate with a large lettuce leaf first to add flare to the presentation.*

iTALiAN CUCUMBER and TOMATO SALAD

This salad reminds me of the dog days of summer. If you live in a place where it's forever summer (you lucky things!) enjoy this salad year round.

2 medium English cucumbers, cut into 1/2-inch (1 cm) dice
1 small red onion, thinly sliced
1 rib celery, finely diced
1/3 cup (80 mL) extra virgin olive oil
1/4 cup (60 mL) red wine vinegar
1 Tbsp (15 mL) finely chopped fresh oregano
1 Tbsp (15 mL) finely chopped fresh basil
1 clove garlic, finely grated
Kosher salt and freshly ground black pepper to taste
4 large heirloom tomatoes, cut into chunks
Shaved Parmesan cheese (optional)

THE RAINFORD METHOD

1. Toss the cucumbers with the red onion, celery, olive oil, vinegar, oregano, basil, garlic and salt and pepper in a salad bowl until well combined.
2. Gently stir in the tomatoes (to avoid breakage). Cover and refrigerate for 2 hours.
3. Stir the salad again just before serving and sprinkle with Parmesan.

Makes 8 servings

JAMAiCAN CHOCOLATE FONDUE

Easy can be fun. I enjoy this recipe because after all the hard work of cooking the main course, all you have to do is melt a little chocolate and dessert's done.

1 cup (250 mL) 35% whipping cream
8 oz (250 g) unsweetened chocolate, chopped
8 oz (250 g) milk chocolate, chopped
¼ cup (60 mL) dark rum (I use Appleton Estate Reserve Dark Rum)
Assorted dippers, such as pineapple chunks, strawberries, figs, ladyfingers,
    cubed pound cake and marshmallows (allow 2 pieces of each per person)

THE RAINFORD METHOD

1. Place the cream, unsweetened chocolate and milk chocolate in a fondue pot set over low heat. Stir until chocolate has melted.
2. Stir in rum and place over a candle warmer or low flame.
3. Serve with assorted dippers.

   Makes 8 servings

MY WIFE ROSE has been with me on my culinary journey since the beginning, and one of the first meals I cooked for her was a smoked veal chop which she still loves to this day. As we added to our family, we had to include ingredients and foods in our repertoire our daughters would eat. I love using a lot of spices but I always remember that when in doubt simply add salt and pepper, hence the Salt-and-Pepper Prime Rib. This menu is one of my family's favorites; it's so good that my daughters help out in the kitchen so we can get it to the grill faster.

FOR THE ROSE iN YOUR LiFE

Smoked **VEAL CHOPS** with *Zinfandel*

Charcoal-grilled **SALT-AND-PEPPER PRIME RIB STEAK**

Italian-style **GRILLED POTATOES**

SWISS CHARD with *Cashews and Golden Raisins*

SWEET FENNEL and **CITRUS APPLE SALAD**

SMOKED VEAL CHOPS with ZiNFANDEL

To mop or not to mop that is the question. I believe that whenever a meat lacks natural fat we must do our utmost to make it tender and juicy. With veal being so lean, it's very important to add moisture back into the equation, and applying a mop while the veal smokes does just that.

On the other hand, some people say that opening the smoker too many times to apply the mop will cause the temperature to drop in such a significant way that you'll never maintain a even cooking temperature.

So, to mop or not, it's your call.

8 veal chops, each about 12 oz (375 g)
  and 1 ½ to 2 inches (4 to 5 cm) thick
Canola oil for greasing
2 handfuls wood chips, soaked in water for at
  least 2 hours
1 handful dry wood chips

Wet Rub	Mop (optional)
1 cup (250 mL) fresh sage leaves	¾ cup (185 mL) Ravenswood Zinfandel
½ lemon, juiced	½ cup (125 mL) veal stock,
½ lime, juiced	homemade or store bought
2 Tbsp (30 mL) Ravenswood Zinfandel or any	2 Tbsp (30 mL) olive oil
full bodied red	Large bushy sprigs of fresh sage
5 cloves garlic	
¼ tsp (1 mL) kosher salt	

THE RAINFORD METHOD

1. Combine all the ingredients for the wet rub in a food processor and process until a paste forms. Rub the paste all over the veal chops.
2. Two to 4 hours before you get to the grill, do yourself a favor and put the veal in a resealable plastic bag and let it hang out in the fridge. Remember because the acid component is low you don't have to worry about your meat becoming tough because of the marinade.

▶

3. Pull the veal chops out of the fridge and them bring to room temperature before grilling. This is an important step because you want the internal temperature of the meat to be at the temperature of the outside of the meat to ensure even cooking.

4. If you want to apply a mop to the veal chops while they smoke, stir together the Zinfandel, stock and olive oil in a small bowl.

5. Fire up your charcoal grill and prep the grill for cooking over indirect heat. You need a low temperature of around 200 to 220°F (93 to 105°C) to smoke the veal chops. For gas grills, preheat the grill to low then turn off one burner to achieve indirect heat. Oil the grate with canola oil.

6. Once the grill is heated, make a smoke pouch by placing two parts wet and one part dry wood chips in a foil pouch. Put pouch directly on the heated side of the grill or into the smoker box that comes with most grills these days. Allow to smoke and then place veal on the cooler side of the grill.

7. The veal chops will take 1 to 1 ½ hours to smoke. If you're using the mop, brush it on the veal chops every 30 minutes during smoking, using a fresh sprig of sage each time. Remember, you don't have to cook the veal chops until they're well done; medium-rare (an internal temperature of 135°F/57°C) is fine.

8. As soon as the chops have reached the internal temperature you like, take them off the grill and let them rest for a few minutes before serving.

Makes 8 servings

CHARCOAL-GRiLLED
SALT-and-PEPPER
PRiME RiB STEAK

This is one of my family's favorites. Be generous with both the salt and pepper here because they're the only two ingredients you have to play with.

The steak can be grilled over either charcoal or gas but my preference is charcoal for this one.

¼ cup (60 mL) olive oil
1 onion, sliced
3 cloves garlic
2 ½ lb (1.25 kg) bone-in standing prime rib steak
Canola oil for greasing
Kosher salt and freshly cracked black pepper to taste

THE RAINFORD METHOD

1. Combine the olive oil, onion and garlic in a resealable plastic bag. Add the steak and place in the fridge for 4 hours.
2. Fire up your charcoal grill and prep the grill for cooking over indirect heat. You need a medium-high temperature of around 350 to 400°F (180 to 200°C) to grill the steak. For gas grills, preheat the grill to medium-high then turn off one burner to achieve indirect heat. Oil the grate with canola oil.
3. Remove the steak from the bag and season generously with salt and pepper. Sear both sides of the prime rib steak, then move the steak to the cooler part of the grill to finish cooking. To get to an internal temperature of 125°F (52°C) for rare meat should take just under 1 hour. Remove the steak from the grill and let it rest for 10 to 15 minutes before slicing.

Makes 6 to 8 servings

iTALiAN-STYLE GRiLLED POTATOES

This recipe is perfect for entertaining because the potatoes can be prepared ahead of time then finished quickly right before serving.

2 lb (1 kg) Yukon gold potatoes, washed and cut into wedges
Kosher salt to taste
¼ cup (60 mL) olive oil
2 Tbsp (30 mL) white wine
2 Tbsp (30 mL) paprika
2 Tbsp (30 mL) finely chopped fresh parsley
4 cloves garlic, finely grated
1 tsp (5 mL) dried basil leaves
¾ tsp (4 mL) dried oregano leaves
Freshly ground black pepper to taste
Canola oil for greasing

THE RAINFORD METHOD

1. Place the potatoes in a pot and cover with cold water and add salt to taste. Bring to a boil and cook for 15 minutes or until al dente. Drain well and arrange the potatoes in a single layer on a baking sheet. Let cool slightly.
2. Meanwhile, whisk the olive oil with the wine, paprika, parsley, garlic, basil and oregano in a large bowl until well combined. Add the potatoes and toss with the oil mixture, seasoning with salt and pepper to taste.
3. Fire up your charcoal or preheat your gas grill. You need a medium-low grilling temp of around 300°F (150°C). Prep the grill for cooking over direct heat. Oil the grate with canola oil.
4. Place the potatoes on the grill and cook, turning occasionally, for 3 to 4 minutes or until well marked and fork tender.

Makes 6 to 8 servings

 Tip: *For best results, undercook the potatoes slightly in step 1 to avoid overcooking them when you finish them on the grill.*

SWISS CHARD with CASHEWS and GOLDEN RAISINS

Who'd have thought of serving Swiss chard with a barbecue? Well, I did and you'll really enjoy this flavorful side. It's got all the elements I'd ever want in one dish: sweet, crunchy and soft.

2 lb (1 kg) Swiss chard, stems discarded and leaves sliced
3 Tbsp (45 mL) olive oil
1 onion, finely diced
½ cup (125 mL) golden raisins
¼ cup (60 mL) roasted cashews, coarsely chopped
¼ tsp (1 mL) ground cinnamon
Kosher salt and freshly ground black pepper to taste

THE RAINFORD METHOD

1. Fire up your charcoal or preheat your gas grill. You need a medium-high grilling temp of around 350°F (180°C). Prep the grill for cooking over direct heat.
2. Steam the Swiss chard for 2 to 3 minutes using the steamer insert of a double boiler. Drain well. Heat a cast iron skillet on the grill and add the oil. Add the onion and cook until tender but not browned.
3. Add the raisins, cashews and cinnamon. Cook until the cashews are golden and the onion is soft. Add the Swiss chard and salt and pepper to taste. Reduce heat to low and cook for 10 minutes or heated through.

Makes 6 to 8 servings

SWEET FENNEL and CiTRUS APPLE SALAD

2 medium oranges

2 medium grapefruit

¼ cup (60 mL) extra virgin olive oil

2 Tbsp (30 mL) fresh lemon juice

1 Tbsp (15 mL) liquid honey

1 fennel bulb, quartered and thinly sliced

2 Granny Smith apples, cored and cut into
    matchsticks

Kosher salt and freshly ground black pepper
    to taste

1 Tbsp (15 mL) balsamic glaze

Balsamic Glaze

The glaze will keep for 1 week in the fridge. Bring it to room temperature before using. If you store it in a squeeze bottle in the fridge, place the bottle in a bowl of hot water to warm the glaze up quickly.

1 cup balsamic vinegar

1 small sauce pot

THE RAINFORD METHOD

1. Using a sharp knife, peel the oranges and grapefruit, removing all the pith (that's the white stuff under the skin). Slice the oranges and grapefruit into ⅛-inch (3 mm) thick rounds. Set aside.

2. Whisk the oil with lemon juice and honey in a large bowl. Add the fennel and apples and toss with the oil mixture until well coated. Season with salt and pepper to taste.

3. Arrange the citrus fruit in a large circle on a serving platter, alternating the orange and grapefruit rounds. Season with salt and pepper. Mound the fennel mixture in the center of the circle and spoon any remaining dressing from the bowl over the citrus fruit. Drizzle with the balsamic glaze.

Makes 6 to 8 servings

THE RAINFORD METHOD

1. Place the balsamic vinegar in a small saucepan over low heat. Simmer until the vinegar develops a syrup-like consistency. Simmering time will depend on the width of the saucepan.

2. To test if it's ready, dip a teaspoon into the glaze, making sure to coat the back of the spoon. Let cool slightly then, with your index finger, draw a line through the glaze on the spoon. If the line stays in place, the glaze is ready.

Tip: *Use a sharp chef's knife or a mandoline to slice the fennel very thinly.*

I'M FOREVER FASCINATED by how some meats that start out so tough can, when cooked for a long time, become so mouth-wateringly good. Ribs have been at the top of my To-Eat List for most of my life. On a hot summer day I enjoy heading out to my backyard, sparking up my smoker and getting started on some flavorful ribs. Time on a hot day is at a premium so I like to finish grilling my ribs using indirect heat. They take four or five hours which gives me lots of time to enjoy the day. I like to serve up my ribs with a refreshing slaw and potatoes. Here's to it being warm and sunny no matter where you are in the world.

RIB FEST
AT MY PLACE,
ANYONE?

⑤

Utility **BABY BACK RIBS**

BBQ RIBS with a Southern Touch

Homemade Mayonnaise

Peruvian **POTATO SALAD** with Buttermilk Dressing

SAVOY CABBAGE SLAW

Dark Beer **GUINNESS DRINK**

UTiLiTY BABY BACK RiBS

If you like your ribs extra saucy, remove them from the grill when they're ready, baste them one last time with the barbecue sauce, then throw them back on the grill to make them nice and sticky.

Ribs
5 Tbsp (75 mL) packed brown sugar
3 Tbsp (45 mL) kosher salt
2 Tbsp (30 mL) sweet smoked paprika
4 tsp (20 mL) ancho chili powder
1 Tbsp (15 mL) paprika
1 Tbsp (15 mL) onion powder
1 Tbsp (15 mL) freshly cracked black pepper
2 tsp (10 mL) dried thyme leaves
6 racks baby back ribs, about 6 lb (2.7 kg)
4 medium chunks hickory wood, soaked in
    water for at least 2 hours (if using a
    charcoal grill) or 4 cups (1 L) hickory
    wood chips, soaked in water for at
    least 2 hours (if using a gas grill)

Barbecue Sauce
¾ cup (185 mL) apple cider
½ cup (125 mL) ketchup
3 Tbsp (45 mL) red wine vinegar
1 Tbsp (15 mL) Dijon mustard
2 tsp (10 mL) light soy sauce
1 tsp (5 mL) Worcestershire sauce
1 tsp (5 mL) molasses
½ tsp (2 mL) ancho chili powder
½ tsp (2 mL) ground cumin
½ tsp (2 mL) minced garlic
¼ tsp (1 mL) freshly ground black pepper

THE RAINFORD METHOD

1. For the ribs, stir together the sugar, salt, smoked paprika, chili powder, regular paprika, onion powder, black pepper and thyme. Set aside.
2. With a small, sharp knife, release the edge of the membrane on the back of each rack of ribs. Grasp the edge with needle-nose pliers or a piece of paper towel and peel the membrane off the rack. (If you leave the membrane on, the ribs will be chewy.)
3. Spread the dry rub all over each rack of ribs until completely coated. Make sure you press the dry rub into the meat. This is where your flavor is going to come from. Arrange the ribs in a rib rack, with all the racks facing the same direction. A rib rack has 8 slab compartments, looks like a rack of coat hangers and can be purchased at most barbecue stores.

▶

4. Fire up your charcoal grill and prep the grill for cooking over indirect heat. You need a low temperature of around 250 to 300°F (120 to 150°C) to grill the ribs. For gas grills, preheat the grill to low then turn off one side of the grill to achieve indirect heat. Place a drip tray on the cooler side of the grate and half fill the pan with warm water or the beer of your choice.

5. Drain 2 chunks of hickory, place them on top of the charcoal and set the grate in place. For gas barbecues, place half of the hickory chips in a foil pouch and place the pouch directly on the heated side of the grill. Wait for the hickory to start to smoke.

6. Place the rib racks over indirect heat as far from the heat as possible, with the bone sides facing toward the heat. Close the lid and close the top vent on a charcoal grill about halfway. This will maintain a temperature between 250 and 300°F (120 and 150°C). Cook the ribs for 2 hours.

7. Once the ribs are on, it's time to start working on the barbecue sauce. If you have a side burner this can be done outside. If you don't, go inside and use your stove top to simmer your sauce. Combine all the ingredients in a small saucepan set over medium heat. Simmer for 20 to 30 minutes or until the sauce reaches a glaze consistency. Remove the saucepan from the heat and set aside to cool.

8. The first batch of charcoal should be cooling down after 2 hours. Now is the time to use your chimney starter and get another batch of charcoal lit. Add the remaining wood chunks to the coals to get a little more smoke. If using a gas grill, wrap the remaining chips in foil and place directly on the hotter side of the grate. Close the lid and grill for another 2 hours. Make sure to come back every hour on the hour to check the temperature and to add more charcoal, if necessary.

9. In the last hour of grilling, your ribs will start to show signs of cooking all the way through. When the meat pulls back from the bone, the ribs are almost ready. Baste the ribs with the barbecue sauce during the last 5 to 10 minutes of cooking.

10. I like to tent my ribs before serving, so take them off the grill and let them rest, loosely covered with foil, for 10 minutes.

Makes 4 to 6 servings

BBQ RiBS with a SOUTHERN TOUCH

This is the rib recipe you reach for if you have a big party to feed.

Ribs

3 Tbsp (45 mL) packed brown sugar

2 Tbsp (30 mL) chili powder

2 Tbsp (30 mL) kosher salt

1 Tbsp (15 mL) paprika

2 tsp (10 mL) oregano

1 tsp (5 mL) garlic powder

1 tsp (5 mL) onion powder

1 tsp (5 mL) freshly ground black pepper

8 racks baby back ribs, about 8 lb (3.5 kg)

¼ cup (60 mL) Dijon mustard

2 cups (500 mL) dry apple wood chunks
(if using a charcoal grill) or 2 cups
(500 mL) cherry wood chips, soaked
in water for at least 2 hours (if using
a gas grill)

Barbecue Sauce

1 cup (250 mL) ketchup

⅓ cup (80 mL) cider vinegar

2 Tbsp (30 mL) packed brown sugar

4 tsp (20 mL) light soy sauce

1 Tbsp (15 mL) liquid honey

1 Tbsp (15 mL) molasses

½ tsp (2 mL) minced garlic

THE RAINFORD METHOD

1. For the ribs, stir together the sugar, chili powder, salt, paprika, oregano, garlic powder, onion powder and black pepper. Set aside.
2. With a small, sharp knife, release the edge of the membrane on the back of each rack of ribs. Grasp the edge with needle-nose pliers or a piece of paper towel and peel the membrane off the rack. (If you leave the membrane on, the ribs will be chewy.)
3. Spread the meaty side of each rack with mustard (I find this helps the rub stick to the ribs). Coat the meaty side of the ribs with the dry rub. Make sure you press the dry rub into the meat. This is where your flavor is going to come from.
4. Arrange the ribs in a rib rack, with all the racks facing the same direction. A rib rack has 8 slab compartments, looks like a rack of coat hangers and can be purchased at most barbecue stores.

▶

5. Fire up your charcoal grill and prep the grill for cooking over indirect heat. You need a low temperature of around 250 to 300°F (120 to 150°C) to grill the ribs. For gas grills, preheat the grill to low then turn off one side of the grill to achieve indirect heat. Place a drip tray on the cooler side of the grate and half fill the pan with warm water or the beer of your choice.

6. Add half of the wood chunks to the charcoal and immediately close the lid to maintain the temperature. If using a gas grill, wrap half of the wood chips in a foil pouch and place on the lit side of the grill. Wait for the wood to start to smoke.

7. Place the rib racks over indirect heat as far from the heat as possible, with the bone sides facing toward the heat. Close the lid and close the top vent on a charcoal grill about halfway. This will maintain a temperature of between 250 and 300°F (120 and 150°C). Cook the ribs for 2 hours.

8. The first batch of charcoal should be cooling down after 2 hours. Now is the time to use your chimney starter and get another batch of charcoal lit. Add the remaining wood chunks to the coals to get a little more smoke. If using a gas grill, wrap the remaining chips in foil and place directly on the hotter side of the grate. Close the lid and grill for another 2 hours. Make sure to come back every hour on the hour to check the temperature and to add more charcoal, if necessary.

9. Once your ribs are doing well, you can start making your barbecue sauce. If you have a side burner this can be done outside. If you don't, go inside and use your stove top to simmer your sauce. Combine all the ingredients in a small saucepan set over medium heat. Simmer for about 30 minutes or until the sauce thickens. Remove the saucepan from the heat and set aside to cool.

10. In the last hour of grilling, your ribs will start to show signs of cooking all the way through. When the meat pulls back from the bone, the ribs are almost ready. Baste the ribs with the barbecue sauce during the last 4 to 5 minutes of cooking.

11. I like to tent my ribs before serving, so take them off the grill and let them rest, loosely covered with foil, for 10 minutes.

Makes 8 servings

HOMEMADE MAYONNAISE

1 egg
1 Tbsp (15 mL) lemon juice
1 tsp (5 mL) Dijon mustard
¾ cup (185 mL) extra virgin olive oil
1 tsp (5 mL) kosher salt

THE RAINFORD METHOD

1. In a food processor, combine the egg, lemon juice and mustard.
2. In a steady stream and with the motor running, pour in the extra virgin olive oil.
3. Blend until thick and smooth, and season with salt to taste.
4. The mayonnaise will keep for 2 to 3 days in the refrigerator.

PERUViAN POTATO SALAD
with BUTTERMiLK DRESSiNG

*I leave the purple skins on the Peruvian potatoes because they maintain their color
after cooking which adds a certain something to the dish.*

2 lb (1 kg) Peruvian potatoes, scrubbed

¼ cup (60 mL) apple cider vinegar

½ cup (125 mL) chopped double smoked bacon (approx. 10 slices)

¾ cup (185 mL) buttermilk

½ cup (125 mL) homemade mayonnaise *(see page 58)*

1 Tbsp (15 mL) finely grated garlic

1 Tbsp (15 mL) grainy Dijon mustard

Kosher salt and freshly ground black pepper to taste

2 green onions, thinly sliced

½ sweet red pepper, seeded and diced

½ sweet yellow pepper, seeded and diced

½ cup (125 mL) finely chopped fresh parsley

½ cup (125 mL) finely chopped fresh mint

THE RAINFORD METHOD

1. Place potatoes in a pot, cover with cold water and add salt to taste. Bring to a boil and cook for 30 minutes or until fork tender. Drain well and let cool for 5 minutes. Drizzle with vinegar.

2. Set a skillet over medium heat. Add bacon and cook until crispy. Remove from skillet and drain on a paper-towel-lined plate. Let cool.

3. Whisk buttermilk, mayonnaise, garlic and mustard in a salad bowl. Season with salt and pepper to taste.

4. Add the cooked potatoes and bacon, green onions, red pepper, yellow pepper, parsley and mint. Stir gently until well combined. Season again with salt and pepper to taste.

Makes 6 servings

 Tip: *The warm potatoes are like sponges and will absorb the flavor of the vinegar better than if they were cold.*

DARK BEER GUINNESS DRINK

My mom used to make this unusual combination and it's quite refreshing on a hot summer's day.

2 cans (440 mL each) Guinness stout
1 can (370 mL) evaporated milk
1 can (300 mL) sweetened condensed milk

THE RAINFORD METHOD

1. Whisk Guinness with evaporated milk and condensed milk in a pitcher until well combined. Chill until ice cold.

Makes 6 cups (1.5 L)

SAVOY CABBAGE SLAW

6 cups (1.5 L) thinly sliced Savoy cabbage
    (about ½ medium head)
1/4 cup (60 mL) kosher salt (approx.)
2 Tbsp (30 mL) grapeseed oil
2 Tbsp (30 mL) rice wine vinegar
1 Tbsp (15 mL) liquid honey
3 cloves garlic, finely grated
2 cups (500 mL) grated carrot
1 sweet red pepper, seeded,
    quartered and thinly sliced
Freshly ground black pepper to taste

THE RAINFORD METHOD

1. In a colander, toss the cabbage with the salt. Set the colander in a large bowl and let stand for 1 hour. Rinse the salt off the cabbage by setting the colander under cold, running water. (Taste a small piece to make sure all the salt has been washed off.) Drain well.

2. Whisk together the oil, vinegar, honey and garlic in a salad bowl. Add the cabbage, carrots and red pepper and toss well with the oil mixture. Season with salt and pepper to taste.

Makes 8 servings

MY DAUGHTERS are the most important people to me and cooking for them is both challenging and rewarding. One of them is a very picky eater but this menu is a home run. We often ask them what their ultimate meal would be and short ribs, beef tenderloin and porterhouse steaks always seem to make it onto the list. Asparagus and a green mango salad round out the menu.

AiDEN, LAUREN and ALYSSA'S "GO TO" MEALS

6

MIAMI SHORT RIB SANDWICH *with Smoked Mozzarella*

Brandy-Butter-Infused **GRILLED BEEF TENDERLOIN**

Grilled Thyme and Rosemary **PORTERHOUSE STEAK** *with Roasted Garlic Butter*

GRILLED ASPARAGUS *with Brown-Butter Sage Sauce and Parmesan Shavings*

GREEN MANGO AND TOMATO SALAD

MiAMi SHORT RiB SANDWiCH
with SMOKED MOZZARELLA

Miami-cut short ribs are a thin cut of beef rib. For best results they should be approximately ¼ inch (6 mm) thick. Ask your butcher for these.

Short Ribs

⅓ cup (80 mL) low-sodium soy sauce

⅓ cup (80 mL) mirin
     (sweet cooking rice wine)

⅓ cup (80 mL) rice wine vinegar

3 Tbsp (45 mL) olive oil (approx.)

1 Tbsp (15 mL) liquid honey

1 tsp (5 mL) hot sauce

3 lb (1.5 kg) Miami-cut short ribs

Sandwiches

2 crusty French baguettes

2 cups (500 mL) shredded smoked mozzarella

Dry Rub

1 ½ tsp (7.5 mL) packed brown sugar

1 ½ tsp (7.5 mL) paprika

1 ½ tsp (7.5 mL) freshly ground black pepper

1 ½ tsp (7.5 mL) garlic powder

1 ½ tsp (7.5 mL) dried oregano leaves

1 ½ tsp (7.5 mL) ground cumin

1 ½ tsp (7.5 mL) dried thyme leaves

1 ½ tsp (7.5 mL) cayenne

1 ½ tsp (7.5 mL) dry mustard

¼ tsp (1 mL) kosher salt (approx.)

THE RAINFORD METHOD

1. For the short ribs, stir together the soy, mirin, rice wine vinegar, 2 Tbsp (30 mL) olive oil, honey and hot sauce in a large bowl until combined. Place the ribs in the marinade mixture and marinate in the fridge for at least 2 hours, or up to 8 hours if time permits.

2. Meanwhile, mix together all the ingredients for the dry rub.

3. Fire up your charcoal or preheat your gas grill. You need a medium-high grilling temp of around 350°F (180°C). Prep the grill for cooking over direct heat.

4. Shake off excess marinade from the ribs and pat them dry with paper towels. Brush the ribs lightly with the remaining olive oil and rub the spice mixture all over the meat.

5. Place ribs on the grill and cook for 5 minutes per side for medium-rare.

6. Trim the rounded ends from each baguette and cut the baguettes in half lengthwise. Remove the bones from the meat and discard. Pile the meat high on the bottom halves of the baguettes and top with the cheese. Replace the tops of the baguettes and cut each into five pieces.

Makes 10 servings

Tip: *Don't skip even the shortest quick marinating time here because a little flavor is better than no flavor.*

Avoid turning ribs too often; the meat will not scorch and will benefit from the direct heat.

BRANDY-BUTTER-iNFUSED GRiLLED BEEF TENDERLOiN

Using an injector can add immense flavor to any meat. I love beef tenderloin and the brandy butter works so well here.

Butter Sauce

6 shallots, thinly sliced

7 Tbsp (105 mL) unsalted butter, melted

2 Tbsp (30 mL) brandy

1 Tbsp (15 mL) finely chopped fresh thyme

2 garlic cloves, coarsely chopped

Kosher salt and freshly ground
  black pepper to taste

Dry Rub

3 Tbsp (45 mL) smoked paprika

4 tsp (20 mL) onion powder

1 Tbsp (15 mL) garlic powder

1 Tbsp (15 mL) kosher salt

1 Tbsp (15 mL) freshly ground black pepper

1 ½ tsp (7.5 mL) chili powder

Beef

5 lb (2.2 kg) beef tenderloin, silver skin removed

3 Tbsp (45 mL) olive oil

Canola oil for greasing

THE RAINFORD METHOD

1. For the butter sauce, place the shallots, butter, brandy, thyme, garlic, and salt and pepper to taste in a blender. Process until smooth and well combined. Transfer half the mixture to a flavor injector, reserving remaining mixture for basting.

2. Pat the tenderloin dry with paper towels. Inject the tenderloin in several areas with the shallot mixture in the flavor injector. Cover tightly with plastic wrap and refrigerate for 2 hours.

3. Combine the paprika, onion powder, garlic powder, salt, pepper and chili powder.

4. Brush the tenderloin with the olive oil and coat with the dry rub, massaging it into the meat. Set aside at room temperature for 30 minutes.

5. Fire up your charcoal grill and prep the grill for cooking over indirect heat. You need a medium-high temperature of around 350°F (180°C) to grill the tenderloin. For gas grills, preheat the grill to medium-high then turn off one burner to achieve indirect heat. Oil the grate with canola oil.

6. Place the tenderloin on the grill over direct heat to sear it for about 4 minutes per side.

7. Move the tenderloin to the cooler part of the grill and baste it with the reserved butter sauce. Close the lid and cook for 12 to 15 minutes for medium-rare to medium, continuing to baste every few minutes. Remove from the grill and let rest for 5 minutes before slicing.

Makes 6 to 8 servings

GRiLLED THYME and ROSEMARY PORTERHOUSE STEAK with ROASTED GARLiC BUTTER

4 Porterhouse steaks,
    each about 12 to 16 oz (375 to 500 g)
    and 1 inch (2.5 cm) thick
8 Tbsp (120 mL) olive oil
½ cup (125 mL) finely chopped fresh thyme
4 Tbsp (60 mL) finely chopped
    fresh rosemary
Kosher salt and freshly ground
    black pepper to taste

THE RAINFORD METHOD

1. Fire up your charcoal grill and prep the grill for cooking over indirect heat. You need a medium-high temperature of around 350°F (180°C) to grill the steaks. For gas grills, preheat the grill to medium-high then turn off one burner to achieve indirect heat.
2. Brush the oil on both sides of each steak. Mix together the thyme, rosemary and salt and pepper to taste. Sprinkle the herb mixture evenly all over the steaks.
3. Place the steaks on the grill over direct heat. Cook for 6 to 8 minutes per side. Move the steaks to the cooler part of the grill and close the lid. Cook for 30 minutes for medium-rare, or to desired doneness.
4. Remove the steaks from the grill and let rest for 5 minutes before cutting each in half. Serve with Roasted Garlic Butter.

Makes 6 to 8 servings

Roasted Garlic Butter
½ cup (125 mL) unsalted butter at room
    temperature
2 Tbsp (30 mL) finely chopped fresh parsley
2 Tbsp (30 mL) roasted garlic (see Tip)
1 tsp (5 mL) finely grated lemon zest
1 Tbsp (15 mL) fresh lemon juice
1 tsp (5 mL) grainy Dijon mustard

THE RAINFORD METHOD

1. Beat the butter on low speed using a mixer fitted with a paddle attachment, until it is smooth and creamy.
2. Add the parsley, roasted garlic, lemon zest and juice and mustard. Beat on low speed until well combined.
3. Divide the butter into quarters and, using a sheet of wax paper to roll each one, form each into a cylinder, about 1 inch (2.5 cm) thick. Wrap in wax paper then in plastic wrap. Place in the fridge until firm.

Makes about 1/2 cup (125 mL)

Tip: *To roast garlic, cut the top off a whole bulb, drizzle with oil and wrap in foil. Roast at 400°F (200°C) for 30 minutes or until tender. Use a fork to remove the cloves from their skins or squeeze the bulb gently.*

GRiLLED ASPARAGUS
with BROWN-BUTTER SAGE SAUCE
and PARMESAN SHAViNGS

Peeling the asparagus before cooking takes a bit more effort but makes for a much prettier presentation.

2 lb (1 kg) asparagus

1 Tbsp (15 mL) olive oil

Kosher salt and freshly ground black pepper to taste

6 Tbsp (90 mL) unsalted butter

¼ cup (60 mL) vegetable broth

3 Tbsp (45 mL) finely chopped fresh sage

1 wedge Parmesan cheese

THE RAINFORD METHOD

1. Snap the woody ends off the asparagus and discard. Run a vegetable peeler down the asparagus stalks to remove the skin. Toss the asparagus with the oil and salt and pepper to taste.

2. Fire up your charcoal or preheat your gas grill. You need a medium-high grilling temp of around 350°F (180°C). Prep the grill for cooking over direct heat.

3. Place the asparagus on the grill and cook, turning often, for 5 minutes or until tender and well marked.

4. Set a medium skillet over medium-high heat. Add the butter and cook for 4 to 5 minutes or until the white foam has evenly browned. Add the vegetable broth and sage, then simmer until the mixture has reduced by half. Season with salt and pepper to taste.

5. Arrange the grilled asparagus on a platter and pour the butter sauce over the top. Shave a generous amount of Parmesan from the wedge and scatter over the asparagus.

Makes 8 servings

Tip: *Use a vegetable peeler to make large Parmesan shavings.*

GREEN MANGO and TOMATO SALAD

Simple salads are so refreshing. This green mango and tomato combo is a definite crowd-pleaser.

1/4 cup (60 mL) fresh lime juice

2 Tbsp (30 mL) packed brown sugar

2 Tbsp (30 mL) fish sauce

1 Tbsp (15 mL) olive oil

1 Tbsp (15 mL) finely grated fresh ginger

2 cloves garlic, finely grated

2 tsp (10 mL) Sriracha sauce (Thai chili sauce)

2 green (unripened) mangoes, peeled, pitted and cut into matchsticks

1 ripe mango, peeled, pitted and cut into matchsticks

2 cups (500 mL) bean sprouts, trimmed

1 cup (250 mL) cashews, coarsely chopped

10 cherry tomatoes, halved

1/2 cup (125 mL) coarsely chopped fresh cilantro

1/3 cup (80 mL) coarsely chopped fresh basil

4 green onions, sliced

1 serrano chili, seeded and diced

1 head iceberg lettuce, cut into 6 wedges

THE RAINFORD METHOD

1. Whisk together the lime juice, sugar, fish sauce, olive oil, ginger, garlic and Sriracha sauce in a small bowl until well combined and sugar has dissolved.
2. Combine the mangoes, bean sprouts, cashews, tomatoes, cilantro, basil, green onions, chili and dressing in a large bowl and toss until well coated.
3. Arrange the iceberg lettuce down the center of a serving platter and mound the salad on top of the lettuce.

Makes 6 servings

IT'S NO SECRET that I was born in Jamaica but what people may not know is that I love to eat the foods of my youth. I've been experimenting for years kicking Jamaican food up a notch. This menu is my version of "home." I've taken some of the standards—strip steaks, jerk shrimp and patties—and put a reggae/Jamaican twist on them. I finished the menu off with some grilled cornbread and Jamaican rice and peas.

They say you can never go home again but this menu shows that it's possible to do the next best thing, and that's to walk over to the barbecue and start making home come to you.

GOiNG HOME

JERK SHRIMP *Inferno*

Plank-grilled **JAMAICAN BEEF PATTIES**

Jamaica Meets **NEW YORK STRIP STEAK**

Grilled **CORNBREAD**

Jamaican **RICE AND PEAS**

JERK SHRIMP INFERNO

The beauty of this particular recipe is that you can serve the shrimp as an appetizer or an entrée. Either way, it takes no time at all for the shrimp to cook and they're guaranteed to be a hit!

To serve the shrimp as an appetizer, thread them onto soaked wooden skewers before grilling, or simply arrange the cooked shrimp on a platter.

1 ¾ cups (435 mL) Jerk Marinade *(see Rainford's Staple Recipes, page xvii)*
60 medium shrimp (16/20 count), peeled and deveined (about 3 lb/1.5 kg)
Canola oil for greasing

THE RAINFORD METHOD

1. Combine the Jerk Marinade and shrimp and marinate for 15 to 30 minutes.
2. Fire up your charcoal or preheat your gas grill. You need a medium-high grilling temp of around 350°F (180°C). Prep the grill for cooking over direct heat. Oil the grate with canola oil.
3. Remove the shrimp from the marinade and shake off the excess. Place the shrimp on the grill in an even layer. Cook for 2 to 4 minutes, turning once halfway through, or until shrimp turn from grey to pink in color.

Makes 8 appetizer servings or 4 main-course servings

Tip: *For an authentic West Indian entrée, serve the shrimp on a bed of fluffy rice. Add some color and flavor by stirring some chopped parsley and finely diced shallots and sweet red peppers into the rice during the last 5 minutes of cooking.*

To continue this simple theme, open up a bag of fresh Asian slaw and toss it with your choice of bottled light-tasting vinaigrette.

PLANK-GRILLED JAMAICAN BEEF PATTIES

Patty Dough

2 cups (500 mL) all-purpose flour

½ tsp (2 mL) Jamaican curry powder

¼ tsp (1 mL) kosher salt

¼ cup (60 mL) cold unsalted butter,
    cut into small cubes

¼ cup (60 mL) cold shortening,
    cut into small cubes

⅓ cup (80 mL) ice water

Beef Patty Filling

2 Tbsp (30 mL) olive oil

1 onion, grated

8 oz (250 g) ground beef-

8 oz (250 g) ground veal

1 tsp (5 mL) Jamaican curry powder

1 tsp (5 mL) finely chopped fresh thyme

1 tsp (5 mL) kosher salt

1 tsp (5 mL) freshly ground black pepper

½ cup (125 mL) beef broth

⅓ cup (80 mL) dry breadcrumbs

3 egg yolks, lightly beaten

2 thin untreated cedar planks,
    soaked in cold water for 2 to 4 hours

THE RAINFORD METHOD

1. For the patty dough, blend the flour with the curry powder and salt until well combined. Add the butter, shortening and water. Blend by hand (or in a food processor using on-off pulses) until the dough is crumbly with pea-size pieces. Be careful not to overmix.

2. Shape the dough into a ball, wrap with plastic wrap and place in the fridge for 1 ½ to 2 hours or until firm.

3. For the beef patty filling, heat the oil in a large skillet set over medium-high heat. Add the onion and cook for 5 minutes or until tender but not browned. Add the ground beef and veal, curry powder, thyme, salt and pepper. Cook for 5 minutes or until meat is browned. Stir in the broth and breadcrumbs, and cook until the mixture resembles a thick paste. Let cool completely.

4. To assemble the patties, roll the dough out to ⅛ inch (3 mm) thickness and cut into 3-inch (8 cm) rounds.

5. Place an equal amount of the beef mixture in the center of each piece of dough. Brush beaten egg yolk over half the exposed dough. Fold the dough over to enclose the filling and pinch the edges to seal the patties. Brush the tops with remaining egg.

6. Fire up your charcoal grill and prep the grill for cooking over indirect heat. You need a medium temperature of around 325°F (160°C) to grill the patties. For gas grills, preheat the grill to medium then turn off one burner to achieve indirect heat.

7. Place planks on the grill over indirect heat for 3 to 5 minutes or until dry.

8. Place the patties on the planks and set on the cooler part of the grill. Cook for 30 to 40 minutes or until golden brown.

Makes about 20 cocktail-size patties

JAMAICA MEETS NEW YORK STRIP STEAK

This is a New York strip with a Jamaican-style rub. Allspice is a key ingredient in most Jamaican recipes.

4 Tbsp (60 mL) extra finely ground Jamaican Blue Mountain Coffee
4 Tbsp (60 mL) packed brown sugar
½ tsp (2 mL) ground allspice
Kosher salt and freshly ground black pepper to taste
8 New York strip steaks, each about 8 oz (250 g) and 1 inch (2.5 cm) thick
Canola oil for greasing

THE RAINFORD METHOD

1. Combine the coffee, brown sugar, allspice and salt and pepper to taste. Pat the rub on both sides of each steak.
2. Fire up your charcoal grill and prep the grill for cooking over indirect heat. You need a medium-high temperature of around 350°F (180°C) to grill the steaks. For gas grills, preheat the grill to medium-high then turn off one burner to achieve indirect heat.
3. Grease the grate with canola oil. Place the steaks on the grill over direct heat. Cook for 4 to 5 minutes per side or until well marked. Move the steaks to the cooler part of the grill and close the lid. Cook for 2 to 3 minutes for medium-rare, or to desired doneness.
4. Remove the steaks from the grill and let rest for 5 minutes before serving.

Makes 8 servings

GRiLLED CORNBREAD

"You gon' to eat yo' cornbread?" is one of my favorite lines from Life, a movie starring Eddie Murphy and Martin Lawrence. I think about it—and chuckle—every time I make this recipe.

½ cup (125 mL) unsalted butter
⅔ cup (160 mL) granulated sugar
2 eggs
1 cup (250 mL) buttermilk
½ tsp (2 mL) baking soda
1 cup (250 mL) extra-fine cornmeal
1 cup (250 mL) all-purpose flour
½ tsp (2 mL) kosher salt

THE RAINFORD METHOD

1. Fire up your charcoal grill and prep the grill for cooking over indirect heat. You need a medium-high temperature of around 350°F (180°C) to grill the cornbread. For gas grills, preheat the grill to medium-high then turn off one burner to achieve indirect heat.
2. Grease a 9- x 5-inch (2 L) loaf pan.
3. Melt the butter in a small saucepan. Remove from the heat and stir in the sugar. Whisk in the eggs until well combined.
4. Transfer the mixture to a bowl and stir in the buttermilk and baking soda until well combined.
5. Stir in the cornmeal, flour and salt until mostly combined with only a few lumps. Pour the batter into the prepared pan.
6. Place the pan on the cooler part of the grill and close the lid. Cook for 30 to 40 minutes or until a wooden skewer inserted into the center comes out clean. Let the cornbread cool for 5 minutes in the pan on a wire rack, then turn out of pan and serve warm cut into slices.

Makes 8 servings

JAMAiCAN RiCE and PEAS

It's a Jamaican thing to use the word "peas" instead of "beans" for this particular recipe. In culinary terms, the word "beans" is correct, but I've left it as "peas" here so my grandmother doesn't roll over in her grave! This recipe can be prepared inside on the stove top or on the side burner of a gas grill.

1 cup (250 mL) dry red kidney beans

3 cups (750 mL) long-grain Converted white rice, washed,
    soaked in water for 1 to 2 hours and drained

½ cup (125 mL) unsweetened coconut milk

2 green onions

1 Scotch bonnet chili

1 sprig fresh thyme

Kosher salt and freshly ground black pepper to taste

THE RAINFORD METHOD

1. Soak the beans in 2 cups (500 mL) water overnight. Drain the beans well and place in a saucepan with enough fresh water to cover them. Bring to a boil over high heat, then reduce heat and cook for at least 4 hours. Drain well.

2. Place 6 cups (1.5 L) water in a large saucepan set over medium heat. Add kidney beans, rice, coconut milk, green onions, whole Scotch bonnet pepper, thyme, and salt and pepper to taste.

3. Bring to a boil then cook for 15 to 20 minutes or until the rice and the red kidney beans are tender. Discard Scotch bonnet chili before serving.

Makes 10 servings

Tip: *Wrap the Scotch bonnet chili in a piece of cheesecloth and tie with string so it won't break up during cooking and can be removed easily.*

You can substitute coconut milk with ½ cup (125 mL) coconut cream, found at West Indian grocery stores. You can use canned kidney beans if it's easier for you, and just skip Step 1 of the Rainford Method.

THIS MENU MADE ME THINK about one of my crazy days working in a French bistro in Toronto. I was fresh out of George Brown College and right at the beginning of my culinary journey. The task that day was to cater an off-site wedding and get through a busy service in the restaurant.

Part of the job of a chef is to find ways to embellish a recipe. This menu takes me back to that early spring day because I had to cook a brisket perfectly for the wedding, and finish prepping sweetbreads for the restaurant's patrons. It was a great day.

TO BOLDLY GO
WHERE NOT MANY
HAVE GONE
BEFORE

8

Barbecue **SLOW-GRILLED BRISKET** *with Southwestern Flavors*

Grilled **BEEF TENDERLOIN** *with Chanterelle* **MUSHROOM STUFFING**

GRILLED SWEETBREADS

Grilled Herb **POTATO FRIES**

JACK-A-RITA!

BARBECUE SLOW-GRILLED BRISKET
with SOUTHWESTERN FLAVORS

This brisket takes 12 to 16 hours to cook so the recipe is not for the faint of heart, but it's well worth the time and effort.

3 Tbsp (45 mL) packed brown sugar

3 Tbsp (45 mL) garlic powder

3 Tbsp (45 mL) onion powder

3 Tbsp (45 mL) paprika

1 Tbsp (15 mL) Cajun seasoning

2 tsp (10 mL) cayenne

2 tsp (10 mL) kosher salt

2 tsp (10 mL) freshly cracked black pepper

10 lb to 15 lb (4.5 to 6.75 kg) beef brisket, some fat trimmed

THE RAINFORD METHOD

1. Stir together the sugar, garlic powder, onion powder, paprika, Cajun seasoning, cayenne, salt and pepper. Rub the mixture all over the brisket, making sure to cover the entire surface.
2. Place the brisket in a large, shallow dish, cover with plastic wrap and place in the fridge for 24 hours.
3. Fire up your charcoal grill and prep the grill for cooking over indirect heat. You need a medium-high temperature of around 350°F (180°C) to sear the brisket. For gas grills, preheat the grill to medium-high then turn off one side of the grill to achieve indirect heat. Place a drip tray on the cooler side of the grate and half fill the pan with warm water or the beer of your choice.

▶

 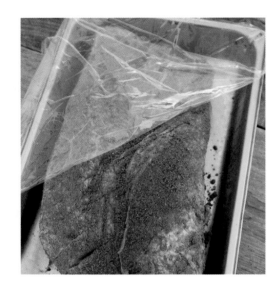

4. Sear the brisket on all sides, then drop the temperature to 220°F (104°C) by leaving the vents slightly open on a charcoal grill, or by reducing the temperature on a gas grill. Cook the brisket for 12 to 16 hours, checking the temperature every 30 minutes and adding more unlit charcoal to a charcoal grill when necessary.

5. You will know the brisket is ready when it reaches an internal temperature of 190°F (88°C). Remove the brisket from the grill, allow it to rest for 15 minutes, then slice and enjoy.

Makes 10 to 12 servings

GRiLLED BEEF TENDERLOiN
with CHANTERELLE MUSHROOM STUFFiNG

5 lb (2.2 kg) beef tenderloin

2 Tbsp (30 mL) olive oil (approx.)

2 cups (500 mL) sliced chanterelle mushrooms

¼ cup (60 mL) dry white wine

2 Tbsp (30 mL) finely chopped shallots

2 Tbsp (30 mL) coarsely chopped fresh thyme, divided

1 Tbsp (15 mL) finely chopped parsley

1 Tbsp (15 mL) white truffle oil

2 cloves garlic, finely chopped

Kosher salt and freshly cracked black pepper to taste

THE RAINFORD METHOD

1. Make a deep incision down the length of the tenderloin so that it opens like a book. Place the tenderloin between 2 pieces of plastic wrap. Pound the meat with a mallet or heavy-bottomed saucepan to make it an even thickness.

2. Fire up your charcoal grill and prep the grill for cooking over indirect heat. You need a medium-high temperature of around 350°F (180°C). For gas grills, preheat the grill to medium-high then turn off one burner to achieve indirect heat.

3. Set a skillet on the grill over direct heat. Add 2 Tbsp (30 mL) oil and heat until smoking. Add the chanterelles, white wine, shallots, 1 Tbsp (15 mL) thyme, the parsley, truffle oil, garlic, and salt and pepper to taste. Cook for 5 minutes or until tender. Remove skillet from grill and let the stuffing cool to room temperature.

4. Arrange the stuffing down the center of the tenderloin. Close the tenderloin and secure it with 8 to 10 pieces of butcher's twine, tied at even intervals.

5. Brush the outside of the tenderloin with additional olive oil, sprinkle with the remaining thyme and season with salt and pepper to taste.

6. Place the tenderloin on the grill over direct heat to sear for about 2 to 3 minutes per side. Move the tenderloin to the cooler part of the grill and close the lid. Cook for 5 minutes or until it reaches an internal temperature of 135°F (57°C) for medium-rare.

7. Remove the tenderloin from the grill and let it rest for 5 minutes before slicing.

Makes 8 to 10 servings

 **Tip:** *Two-tiered heat is the best way to cook this beef.*

GRiLLED SWEETBREADS

Begin preparations for this recipe a day ahead. Starting early will give the sweetbreads time to firm up, which allows them to keep their shape once placed on the grill.

8 cups (2 L) cold water
2 lemons, halved
4 Tbsp (60 mL) kosher salt
2 bay leaves
2 lb (1 kg) sweetbreads
4 eggs, beaten
1 cup (250 mL) all-purpose flour
20 wooden skewers, soaked in water for 2 hours
2 Tbsp (30 mL) olive oil

THE RAINFORD METHOD

1. Bring the water to a boil and add the lemons, salt and bay leaves. Add the sweetbreads to the water and simmer for 5 minutes or until firm. Remove the sweetbreads from the water. When cool enough to handle, peel off and discard the thin membranes.
2. Wrap the sweetbreads in plastic wrap. Place in a flat-bottomed container. Top with a second container of similar shape that fits inside the first container so it can sit directly on top of the sweetbreads. Place a weight on top of the second container. Refrigerate overnight.
3. Fire up your charcoal or preheat your gas grill. You need a medium-high grilling temp of around 350°F (180°C). Prep the grill for cooking over direct heat.
4. Unwrap the sweetbreads and slice them lengthwise into 1 ½-inch (4 cm) thick pieces. Dip the pieces in the beaten egg and coat evenly in flour. Thread them onto the soaked wooden skewers.
5. Brush the sweetbreads lightly with olive oil. Cook for 6 to 8 minutes, turning once, until golden brown.

Makes 8 to 10 servings

JACK-A-RiTA!

*This recipe is an easy one. This delicious
Southwestern cocktail was inspired by
my university days in Ottawa!*

8 oz Jack Daniel's Tennessee Whiskey
4 oz Grand Marnier
3 oz blue curaçao
2 oz grenadine
Lots of ice
Lime margarita mix

THE RAINFORD METHOD

1. Place the whiskey, Grand Marnier,
   curaçao and grenadine in a blender
   filled with ice. Top up generously with
   the lime margarita mix and blend
   until smooth.
2. Pour into margarita glasses and enjoy!

Makes 4 large cocktails

GRiLLED HERB POTATO FRiES

1 lb (500 g) sweet potatoes, peeled and cut into 1-inch (2.5 cm) thick fingers

1 lb (500 g) Yukon gold potatoes, peeled and cut into 1-inch (2.5 cm) thick fingers

Kosher salt to taste

1 lemon, zested and juiced (zest and juice kept separate)

½ cup (125 mL) finely chopped fresh parsley

¼ cup (60 mL) finely chopped fresh chives

3 Tbsp (45 mL) olive oil

2 garlic cloves, finely grated

Freshly ground black pepper to taste

Canola oil for greasing

THE RAINFORD METHOD

1. Place sweet potatoes and Yukon gold potatoes in a large pot, cover with cold water and add salt to taste. Bring to a boil and cook for 12 to 15 minutes or until tender-crisp. Drain well and let cool for 5 minutes. Drizzle with the lemon juice.

2. Place lemon zest, parsley, chives, oil and garlic in a mortar and pound with the pestle until a paste forms (or pulse in a food processor).

3. Transfer paste to a large bowl. Add the potatoes and toss well. Let stand until ready to grill.

4. Fire up your charcoal or preheat your gas grill. You need a medium-high grilling temp of around 350°F (180°C). Prep the grill for cooking over direct heat. Oil the grate with canola oil.

5. Remove the potatoes from the bowl, reserving any of the herb mixture that's left. Place potatoes on the grill and cook, turning often, for 5 to 10 minutes or until well marked on all sides and cooked through.

6. Return the potatoes to the large bowl and toss to coat with the remaining herb mixture.

Makes 8 servings

I'M OFTEN OUT ON THE ROAD throughout the year promoting something, and I've had the opportunity to travel quite extensively over the past 10 years. Sounds exotic? Well, to be honest, it means lots of early mornings and late nights. As a consolation prize we chefs get our perks by eating in some of the best places.

This menu reflects the time when I cooked for a former prime minister of Malaysia. I remember having a discussion with him about all the things that influence food both in his country and in Canada. We agreed that it's wonderful when cooking and eating are shaped by cultures merging together.

For this menu, I drew from my experiences in Asia, and have tied in Szechuan chicken, the Malaysian satays I had on the streets of Kuala Lumpur, and baby bok choy grilled with sesame.

ON THE ROAD AGAIN

CHICKEN THIGHS *Szechuan-Style*

Grilled **MALAYSIAN SATAY** *with Peanut Sauce*

Grilled Sesame **BABY BOK CHOY**

CHICKPEA AND TOMATO SALAD *with Yellow Pepper*

ARUGULA, FRISÉE *and* **CHERRY TOMATO SALAD** *with Champagne Vinaigrette*

CHiCKEN THiGHS SZECHUAN-STYLE

Serve these flavorful chicken thighs with jasmine rice and grilled bok choy.

½ cup (125 mL) hoisin sauce, divided

6 Tbsp (90 mL) light soy sauce, divided

2 Tbsp (30 mL) freshly ground Szechuan peppercorns

2 Tbsp (30 mL) finely grated fresh ginger

4 cloves garlic, finely grated

2 tsp (10 mL) star anise powder

2 tsp (10 mL) granulated sugar

1 tsp (5 mL) chili powder

16 skin-on, boneless chicken thighs

4 Tbsp (60 mL) grapeseed oil

2 cups (500 mL) diced onion

1 sweet red pepper, seeded and diced

2 Tbsp (30 mL) rice wine vinegar

2 tsp (10 mL) sambal oelek (hot chili sauce)

Kosher salt and freshly ground black pepper to taste

THE RAINFORD METHOD

1. Place ¼ cup (60 mL) hoisin sauce, 4 Tbsp (60 mL) soy sauce, Szechuan pepper, ginger, garlic, star anise powder, sugar and chili powder in a resealable plastic bag. Add the chicken and give it a good massage through the bag. Place in the fridge to marinate for 6 to 8 hours.

2. Heat the oil in a medium saucepan set over medium heat. Add the onion and cook for 5 minutes or until tender. Add the red pepper and continue to cook until tender.

3. Add the remaining hoisin and soy sauces, vinegar and sambal oelek. Simmer until reduced by half, then set aside.

4. Fire up your charcoal or preheat your gas grill. You need a medium-high grilling temp of around 350°F (180°C). Prep the grill for cooking over direct heat.

5. Remove the chicken from the marinade and season with salt and pepper. Place the chicken on the grill and cook for 20 to 22 minutes, turning and brushing with some of the sauce, until well glazed and cooked through. Brush with additional sauce and serve.

Makes 8 servings

GRiLLED MALAYSiAN SATAY with PEANUT SAUCE

Having eaten these in the streets of Kuala Lumpur and Singapore, I had to make them for this cookbook. Thank you to Asian Food Channel for helping me with this one.

1 tsp (5 mL) whole black peppercorns
1 tsp (5 mL) whole coriander seeds
1 tsp (5 mL) whole fennel seeds
1 tsp (5 mL) whole cumin seeds
6 shallots, peeled
2 Tbsp (30 mL) packed brown sugar
3 cloves garlic
1 inch (2.5 cm) fresh ginger, peeled and coarsely chopped
1 tsp (5 mL) turmeric
1 tsp (5 mL) belacan (Malaysian dried shrimp paste)
1 lb (500 g) flank steak or skinless, boneless chicken breasts, cut into strips
16 wooden skewers, soaked in water for 2 hours
¼ cup (60 mL) grapeseed oil
1 Tbsp (15 mL) liquid honey
1 tsp (5 mL) finely chopped lemongrass
Canola oil for greasing
Peanut Sauce *(see page 104)*

THE RAINFORD METHOD

1. Set a small skillet over medium heat. Add the peppercorns and coriander, fennel and cumin seeds. Toast the spices, shaking the skillet often, just until fragrant. Place the mixture in a spice grinder or use a mortar and pestle to grind into a fine powder.
2. Place the ground spices, shallots, sugar, garlic, ginger, turmeric and belacan in a blender. Blend until a smooth paste forms, adding up to 2 Tbsp (30 mL) water if necessary.
3. Combine the beef or chicken strips with the paste in a resealable plastic bag. Refrigerate overnight.
4. Fire up your charcoal or preheat your gas grill. You need a medium-high grilling temp of around 350°F (180°C). Prep the grill for cooking over direct heat.
5. Remove the meat from the marinade, discarding the marinade. Thread one strip of meat onto each skewer, leaving 2 inches (5 cm) at the end for easy handling.
6. Whisk together the grapeseed oil, honey and lemongrass until well combined.
7. Oil the grate with canola oil. Grill the skewers for 3 to 5 minutes, turning and basting often with the oil mixture, until golden brown (and cooked through, if using chicken). Serve with Peanut Sauce.

Makes 8 servings

PEANUT SAUCE

2 shallots, coarsely chopped

2 cloves garlic, coarsely chopped

1 inch (2.5 cm) fresh ginger, peeled and coarsely chopped

½ stalk lemongrass (white part only), coarsely chopped

2 macadamia nuts

½ tsp (2 mL) belacan (Malaysian dried shrimp paste)

⅓ serrano chili, seeded and coarsely chopped

1 ½ cups (375 mL) peanuts, toasted and coarsely chopped

⅓ cup (80 mL) white sesame seeds, toasted

⅓ cup (80 mL) grapeseed oil

1 cup (250 mL) unsweetened coconut milk

¼ cup (60 mL) water

2 Tbsp (30 mL) granulated sugar

1 Tbsp (15 mL) fresh lime juice

Kosher salt to taste

THE RAINFORD METHOD

1. Place the shallots, garlic, ginger, lemongrass, macadamia nuts, belacan and serrano chili in a blender, and process until a smooth paste forms.
2. Toss the peanuts with the sesame seeds in a sturdy plastic bag and pound with a mallet or the bottom of a skillet to release the oils. Set aside.
3. Heat the oil in a small saucepan set over medium heat. Add the paste and cook for 3 to 4 minutes or until toasted and the oil starts to separate. Add the coconut milk, water and sugar. Cook for 5 minutes or until slightly thickened.
4. Add the peanut mixture and cook for 5 to 7 minutes or until the desired consistency is reached. Add the lime juice, and season with salt to taste.

Makes about 3 cups (750 mL)

Tip: *To toast the peanuts and sesame seeds, spread them out on a baking sheet and set on a grill heated to medium heat. Give them a good shake every minute and cook just until they develop a nice toasted color; be careful not to burn them.*

The peanut sauce can be stored in an airtight container for up to 1 week in the fridge.

GRiLLED SESAME BABY BOK CHOY

6 Tbsp (90 mL) water
4 Tbsp (60 mL) soy sauce
2 Tbsp (30 mL) finely grated ginger
2 tsp (10 mL) finely grated garlic
2 tsp (10 mL) granulated sugar
2 tsp (10 mL) sesame oil
2 tsp (10 mL) grapeseed oil
8 baby bok choy, halved lengthwise, washed and drained
Canola oil for greasing
2 Tbsp (30 mL) sesame seeds, toasted

THE RAINFORD METHOD

1. Whisk together the water, soy sauce, ginger, garlic, sugar, sesame oil and grapeseed oil in a large bowl until well combined. Add the bok choy and toss until well coated with the dressing.
2. Fire up your charcoal grill and prep the grill for cooking over indirect heat. You need a high temperature of around 400°F (200°C) to grill the bok choy. For gas grills, preheat the grill to high then turn off one burner to achieve indirect heat. Oil the grate with canola oil.
3. Place the bok choy on the cooler part of the grill and cook for 2 to 3 minutes, turning once, until tender. Place on a platter and sprinkle with sesame seeds.

Makes 8 servings

CHiCKPEA and TOMATO SALAD
with YELLOW PEPPER

2 cans (540 mL each) chickpeas, drained and rinsed

2 plum tomatoes, seeded and diced

1 sweet yellow pepper, seeded and diced

½ red onion, diced

2 lemons, juiced

¼ cup (60 mL) extra virgin olive oil

2 Tbsp (30 mL) finely chopped fresh parsley

2 cloves garlic, minced

Kosher salt and freshly ground black pepper to taste

THE RAINFORD METHOD

1. Toss the chickpeas with the tomatoes, yellow pepper, red onion, lemon juice, olive oil, parsley, garlic, and salt and pepper to taste in a large salad bowl, until well combined.
2. Cover tightly and refrigerate until ready to serve.

Makes 8 servings

ARUGULA, FRISÉE and CHERRY TOMATO SALAD with CHAMPAGNE VINAIGRETTE

1/4 cup (60 mL) Champagne vinegar

2 Tbsp (30 mL) Dijon mustard

1 shallot, chopped

1 tsp (5 mL) finely grated lemon zest

2 Tbsp (30 mL) fresh lemon juice

2 Tbsp (30 mL) liquid honey

1 clove garlic, pushed through a garlic press

1/2 cup (125 mL) extra virgin olive oil

Kosher salt and freshly ground black pepper to taste

1 large head frisée, washed, dried and chopped

4 cups (1 L) lightly packed washed and dried baby arugula

1 cup (250 mL) baby bocconcini cheese

1/2 cup (125 mL) heirloom red cherry tomatoes

1/2 cup (125 mL) heirloom yellow cherry tomatoes

2 Tbsp (30 mL) very thinly sliced fresh basil

THE RAINFORD METHOD

1. Place the Champagne vinegar, mustard, shallot, lemon zest and juice, honey and garlic in a blender. With the motor running, slowly drizzle in the olive oil, blending until mixture is well combined. Season with salt and pepper to taste.

2. Toss the frisée with a small amount of dressing in a large bowl. Arrange the frisée around the outside of a large serving platter.

3. Using the same bowl, toss the arugula with a small amount of dressing. Place the arugula in the center of the platter.

4. Add the bocconcini and tomatoes to the bowl. Add the remaining dressing, basil, and salt and pepper to taste and toss well. Arrange the tomato mixture on top of the arugula.

Makes 8 servings

SOME SAY THE TRUE MARK of a great cook is how well they fix chicken. I'm a fanatic about chicken and, here, I've put together some really interesting combinations, like Bacon-Wrapped Chicken "Chops," smoked chicken thighs and Fired-Up Chicken Wings. I'm not ashamed to say I love chicken wings. I've had them in almost every corner of the earth. So, don't listen to anyone who turns his nose up at wings. I'm not saying I don't also love foie gras; like all foods, it has its place.

To finish off this menu, I've reached for Cucumber and Mango Salad and light summer greens for a dinner that will have you wanting to live out in your backyard all summer long.

WiNGS AND THiNGS

Bacon-Wrapped CHICKEN "CHOPS"

Fired-Up CHICKEN WINGS

When Smoke Gets in Your CHICKEN THIGHS

Sweet-and-Sour CUCUMBER AND MANGO SALAD

RADICCHIO and BOSTON LETTUCE SALAD

BACON-WRAPPED CHiCKEN "CHOPS"

This chicken appetizer is a bit of work but well worth the effort and definitely a Super Bowl-worthy snack. The beauty of these "chops" is they have a built-in "handle" so they can be eaten with one hand. Wicked, I know!

3 lb (1.5 kg) chicken wingettes (about 30) *(see Tip)*
½ sweet red pepper, seeded and finely diced
2 shallots, finely diced
3 large green olives, pitted and finely chopped
15 slices bacon, halved

THE RAINFORD METHOD

1. With a sharp boning knife, make a small incision at one end of each wingette, in between the two bones. Be sure to cut into the same side of each chicken wing.
2. Going through the incision, remove the smaller of the two bones, leaving the larger bone (the "handle") attached to the wingette. Pull the meat back to resemble an inverted umbrella and expose the bone.
3. Toss together the red pepper, shallots and olives. Stuff a small amount of the mixture into the pocket formed by the pulled-back meat of each wingette.
4. Tightly wrap a piece of bacon around each stuffed wingette. Secure with a toothpick and refrigerate until ready to grill.
5. Fire up your charcoal grill and prep the grill for cooking over indirect heat. You need a temperature of around 350°F (180°C) to grill the wingettes. For gas grills, preheat the grill to 350°F (180°C) then turn off one burner to achieve indirect heat.
6. Brown the wingettes evenly over direct heat, then move them to the cooler side of the grill. Cook for 30 to 45 minutes, turning often, or until the juices run clear, the bacon is crisp and the chicken reaches an internal temperature of 170°F (76°C).

Makes about 30 "chops"

Tip: *There are three sections to a chicken wing: the drumette (that resembles a tiny chicken drumstick), the wingette (featured in this recipe) and the tip, which is the piece with hardly any meat on it but which works well in chicken stock.*

A little trick I use to help the wingettes to keep their shape is to wrap them tightly in plastic wrap after you've stuffed them and wrapped them in bacon, then refrigerate them until they're chilled. Remember, a food's appearance is just as important as how it tastes.

FiRED-UP CHiCKEN WiNGS

Anyone who knows me will tell you that my guilty pleasure is eating chicken wings. And I really enjoy them on the grill. Whether they're cooked using charcoal or gas, I will always find a way to make them as tasty as I can. Sometimes I'll play with different types of grills, too. Since my trip to Asia, I've started experimenting with a ceramic kamodo-style grill. This charcoal grill retains heat from the top and the bottom, allowing for even distribution.

½ cup (125 mL) canola oil

¼ cup (60 mL) **Jerk Marinade** *(see Rainford's Staple Recipes, page xvii)*

2 Tbsp (30 mL) chili powder

2 Tbsp (30 mL) onion powder

1 Tbsp (15 mL) garlic powder

1 Tbsp (15 mL) smoked paprika

1 Tbsp (15 mL) freshly ground black pepper

1 jalapeño chili (for less heat, seed the chili)

1 tsp (5 mL) kosher salt

½ tsp (2 mL) ground ginger

2 lb (1 kg) chicken wings

THE RAINFORD METHOD

1. Combine the canola oil, jerk marinade, chili powder, onion powder, garlic powder, smoked paprika, black pepper, jalapeño, salt and ground ginger in a large bowl.
2. Add the chicken wings and toss to coat evenly. Refrigerate for at least 2 hours or up to 24 hours.
3. Fire up your charcoal. You need a medium-high grilling temp of around 350°F (180°C). Prep the grill for cooking over direct heat. If using a gas barbecue, preheat one side to medium-high and turn the other burner off so you can finish grilling the wings on the cooler side of the grill if they start to char.
4. Remove the wings from the marinade, shaking off the excess. Pat the wings dry with paper towels.
5. Grill the wings, turning often, for 20 to 30 minutes or until golden and the juices run clear. (If using a kamado-style grill, the wings need to be turned just once, halfway through cooking.)

Makes 2 main-course servings; 10 appetizer-size servings

When Smoke Gets in Your CHiCKEN THiGHS

I've used my gas grill a lot but as I get older I find myself gravitating toward charcoal. I'm not quite sure if it's the taming of the fire that fires me up (no pun intended) but I'm excited to be out recreating some of my favorite nostalgic flavors over charcoal.

¼ cup (60 mL) fresh lime juice
3 Tbsp (45 mL) olive oil
2 Tbsp (30 mL) Dijon mustard
1 Tbsp (15 mL) liquid honey
½ tsp (2 mL) garlic powder
¼ tsp (1 mL) ground cumin
¼ tsp (1 mL) sweet paprika
12 chicken thighs, skin on and bone in
2 handfuls hickory wood chips, soaked in water for at least 2 hours

THE RAINFORD METHOD

1. Combine the lime juice, oil, mustard, honey, garlic powder, cumin and paprika. Place the chicken thighs in a resealable plastic bag with the marinade and refrigerate for 2 hours.
2. Fire up your charcoal grill and prep the grill for cooking over indirect heat. You need a temperature of around 350°F (180°C) to grill the chicken. For gas grills, preheat the grill to 350°F (180°C) then turn off one burner to achieve indirect heat.
3. Once the charcoal grill is heated, place two handfuls of soaked hickory wood chips on top of the lit charcoal. For gas barbecues, place the hickory chips in a foil pouch and place the pouch directly on the heated side of the grill.
4. Remove the chicken from the marinade and place over the cooler part of the grill. Allow the smoke to penetrate the thighs. Cook for 30 minutes or until cooked through. Move the thighs over direct heat and cook for 6 to 7 minutes per side or until well-marked and the chicken reaches an internal temperature of 170°F (76°C).

Makes 8 servings

Sweet-and-Sour CUCUMBER and MANGO SALAD

2 English cucumbers
1 firm mango, peeled
3 Tbsp (45 mL) fish sauce
3 Tbsp (45 mL) fresh lime juice
3 Tbsp (45 mL) water
2 Tbsp (30 mL) granulated sugar
½ red onion, thinly sliced
½ serrano chili, seeded and thinly sliced

THE RAINFORD METHOD

1. Halve the cucumbers lengthwise. Scrape out the seeds using a spoon, then slice the cucumbers thinly.
2. Slice the mango flesh thinly lengthwise, discarding the pit.
3. Whisk together the fish sauce, lime juice, water and sugar until well combined and the sugar has dissolved.
4. Toss the dressing with the cucumbers, mango, red onion and serrano chili in a large salad bowl until well coated. Let marinate for 15 to 20 minutes before serving.

Makes 4 to 6 servings

RADICCHIO and BOSTON LETTUCE SALAD

6 heads Boston lettuce, washed and dried
4 heads radicchio, washed and dried

Dressing
5 Tbsp (75 mL) fresh lemon juice
2 Tbsp (30 mL) minced shallot
4 tsp (20 mL) granulated sugar
Kosher salt and freshly ground
       black pepper to taste
¾ cup (185 mL) olive oil

THE RAINFORD METHOD

1. Tear the larger lettuce and radicchio leaves into smaller pieces, leaving the smaller leaves whole. Toss the leaves together in a large salad bowl.
2. Whisk together the lemon juice, shallot, sugar and salt and pepper to taste in a small bowl. Add the oil in a slow stream, whisking until the dressing is emulsified.
3. Drizzle the dressing over the salad and toss until well combined.

Makes 10 to 12 servings

ONE SUMMER I had the great honor of being invited to Asia to tour three countries in two-and-a-half weeks. Part of my job is to be an ambassador for barbecue around the world and when I travel abroad and speak to groups, I like to be given a local recipe and leave several of mine behind. This menu reflects that cultural exchange.

From the Rendang recipe which my very good friend chef Michael Pasto reminded me would work on the barbecue, to the Alder-Wood-Smoked Whole Chicken and Grilled Ginger and Parmesan Mini Chicken Meatballs, this menu shows just how versatile chicken can be.

FROM INDONESIA TO NORTH AMERICA IN ONE MENU

Grilled **FENNEL AND GREEN APPLE SOUP**

Grilled **INDONESIAN CHICKEN** (Rendang)

ALDER-WOOD-SMOKED Whole **CHICKEN**

Grilled Ginger and Parmesan **MINI CHICKEN BALLS**

Grilled **ROMAINE SALAD** with Anchovy Vinaigrette

GRiLLED FENNEL and GREEN APPLE SOUP

4 Granny Smith apples, cored and quartered

2 bulbs fennel, cut into thirds

2 shallots, halved

3 Tbsp (45 mL) olive oil

½ cup (125 mL) unsalted butter

¼ cup (60 mL) cider vinegar

3 cloves garlic, minced

4 cups (1 L) vegetable or chicken stock *(see Rainford's Staple Recipes, page xvi)*

½ cup (125 mL) white wine

Kosher salt and freshly ground black pepper to taste

THE RAINFORD METHOD

1. Fire up your charcoal or preheat your gas grill. You need a medium-high grilling temp of around 350°F (180°C). Prep the grill for cooking over direct heat.

2. Toss the apples, fennel and shallots with the oil in a large bowl until evenly coated.

3. Grill the apples, fennel and shallots over direct heat until lightly charred. Remove from the grill. Set aside until cool enough to handle, then chop coarsely.

4. Melt the butter in a large heavy saucepan set over medium heat on the grill or side burner. Add the apples, fennel and shallots. Cook, stirring often, until tender.

5. Add the cider vinegar and garlic. Simmer until slightly reduced. Add the stock and white wine, then simmer for 20 to 30 minutes or until vegetables are very soft. Let cool slightly.

6. Transfer the soup, in batches, to a blender and purée until smooth. Pour through a fine-mesh strainer, discarding any solids. Reheat and season to taste with salt and pepper.

Makes 8 servings

Tip: *For a simple garnish, drizzle the soup with a small amount of extra virgin olive oil. If the soup seems too thin, whisk a splash of 35% whipping cream and an egg yolk into the warm soup. Do not allow the soup to boil during reheating because it will cause the egg to curdle.*

GRILLED INDONESIAN CHICKEN (Rendang)

¾ cup (185 mL) unsweetened coconut milk

1 onion, quartered

¼ cup (60 mL) fish sauce

2 Tbsp (30 mL) finely chopped lemongrass

2 Tbsp (30 mL) dark soy sauce

1 Tbsp (15 mL) packed brown sugar

1 Tbsp (15 mL) ground coriander

1 Tbsp (15 mL) ground cumin

3 cloves garlic, coarsely chopped

2 ½ tsp (12 mL) tamarind paste (see Tip)

1 serrano chili, seeded and coarsely chopped

½ inch (1 cm) fresh ginger, peeled and coarsely chopped

1 tsp (5 mL) ground cinnamon

½ tsp (2 mL) ground turmeric

¼ tsp (1 mL) ground nutmeg

8 boneless chicken breasts with skin

2 Tbsp (30 mL) grapeseed oil

Kosher salt and freshly ground black pepper to taste

Peanut Sauce (see page 104)

THE RAINFORD METHOD

1. Place the coconut milk, onion, fish sauce, lemongrass, soy sauce, sugar, coriander, cumin, garlic, tamarind paste, chili, ginger, cinnamon, turmeric and nutmeg in a food processor or blender. Pulse until smooth.

2. Combine three-quarters of the paste mixture with the chicken in a resealable plastic bag. Marinate overnight in the fridge.

3. Fire up your charcoal or preheat your gas grill. You need a medium-high grilling temp of around 350°F (180°C). Prep the grill for cooking over indirect heat.

4. Remove the chicken from the marinade. Drizzle the chicken with oil and season with salt and pepper to taste. Sear the chicken by placing it skin-side down over direct heat. Cook for about 3 minutes then turn each piece through a quarter turn (from the 12 o'clock position to 3 o'clock). Cook for about 3 minutes or until the skin is golden brown.

5. Move the chicken to the cooler side of the grill and grill for 20 to 25 minutes, brushing with remaining paste mixture and turning once, or until the chicken is well marked and the juices run clear.

6. Serve with Peanut Sauce.

Makes 8 servings

 Tip: *Tamarind paste can be found in the international aisle of most grocery stores.*

ALDER-WOOD-SMOKED WHOLE CHiCKEN

This is the kind of simple-looking recipe that might tempt you to say, "So what." But once you taste the finished product, you'll be asking, "Where can I find some alder wood?"

2 whole chickens, each about 4 lb (1.8 kg)
⅓ cup (80 mL) kosher salt, divided
2 Tbsp (30 mL) unsalted butter, melted
1 tsp (5 mL) freshly ground black pepper
2 large handfuls alder wood chips, soaked in water for at least 2 hours

THE RAINFORD METHOD

1. Tuck the chicken wing tips behind each chicken. Measure out 1 tsp (5 mL) salt and set aside. Sprinkle the remaining salt all over surface of the chickens and inside their cavities. Cover the chickens with plastic wrap and refrigerate for 1 ½ to 2 hours.

2. Rinse the chickens inside and out with cold water. Gently pat dry with paper towels. Brush the chickens all over with melted butter, and season with pepper and remaining salt. Let the chickens sit at room temperature for 20 to 30 minutes.

3. Fire up your charcoal grill and prep the grill for cooking over indirect heat. You need a medium temperature of around 325°F (160°C) to grill the chickens. For gas grills, preheat the grill to medium then turn off one burner to achieve indirect heat.

4. Drain the wood chips and scatter them over the charcoal. For gas barbecues, place the wood chips in a foil pouch and place the pouch directly on the heated side of the grill.

5. When the chips begin to smoke place the chickens, breast side up, over the cooler part of the grill, with their legs facing the hotter side. Close the lid.

6. Cook for 1 ¼ to 1 ½ hours, rotating the chickens as needed for even browning, until chickens reach an internal temperature of 175°F (80°C) in the thickest part of the thigh. Let stand for about 10 minutes before carving.

Makes 8 servings

Tip: *Avoid the temptation to peek, and keep the lid closed as much as possible.*

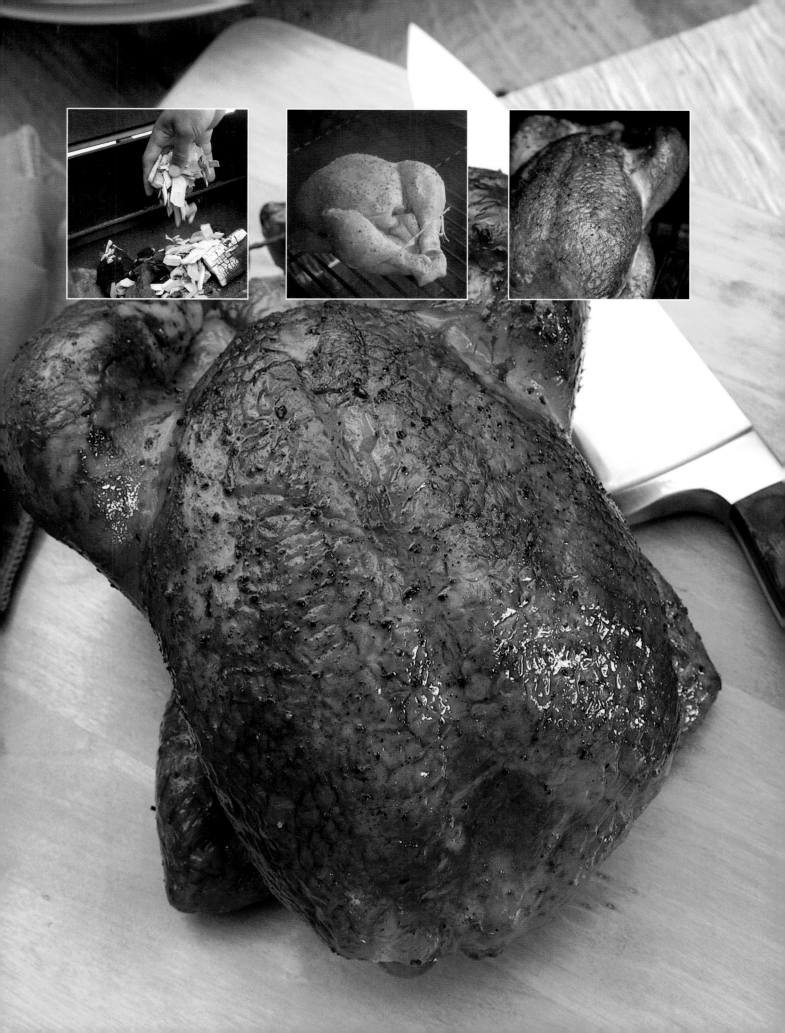

GRiLLED GiNGER and PARMESAN MiNi CHiCKEN MEATBALLS

3 lb (1.5 kg) ground chicken
1 onion, grated
2 ribs celery, grated
6 cloves garlic, finely grated
¼ cup (60 mL) freshly grated
    Parmesan cheese
¼ cup (60 mL) dry breadcrumbs
2 egg yolks
1 Tbsp (15 mL) finely grated fresh ginger
1 tsp (5 mL) Worcestershire sauce
½ tsp (2 mL) hot sauce
Kosher salt and freshly ground

black pepper to taste
Olive oil for brushing
½ cup (125 mL) cherry jelly, melted
¼ cup (60 mL) tomato ketchup
½ jalapeño chili, seeded and chopped
1 tsp (5 mL) minced canned chipotle
    in adobo sauce
½ tsp (2 mL) cider vinegar
¼ tsp (1 mL) fresh lemon juice
24 slider buns, small dinner rolls or sliced
    baguette (2 cm thick)

THE RAINFORD METHOD

1. Gently mix together the ground chicken, onion, celery, garlic, Parmesan, breadcrumbs, egg yolks, ginger, Worcestershire sauce, hot sauce, and salt and pepper to taste. Divide the meat mixture into 24 even-size portions and form into balls. Brush each meatball lightly with oil.

2. Stir together the cherry jelly, ketchup, jalapeño, chipotle, vinegar and lemon juice until well blended and smooth.

3. Fire up your charcoal or preheat your gas grill. You need a medium-high grilling temp of around 350°F (180°C). Prep the grill for cooking over direct heat.

4. Place the meatballs on the grate and cook, turning as needed, for 10 to 12 minutes or until fully cooked but still moist inside. Brush the meatballs with the cherry mixture during the last 5 minutes of grilling.

5. When the meatballs are almost done, toast the rolls on the barbecue until warm and crusty; or brush the baguette slices with olive oil and grill until golden brown.

6. Place 1 meatball in each bun and serve at once.

Makes 8 servings (3 sliders per serving)

 **Tip:** *Don't overwork the ground chicken mixture because it will result in tough meatballs.*

GRiLLED ROMAiNE SALAD
with ANCHOVY ViNAiGRETTE

*I've had thousands of salads in my life and most of them were cold. For a little treat, I took
a second look at an old standby and put my Rainford twist on it. If you like Caesar salads,
you'll really enjoy this one.*

¼ cup (60 mL) olive oil
1 Tbsp (15 mL) balsamic vinegar
1 Tbsp (15 mL) Dijon mustard
1 Tbsp (15 mL) fresh lemon juice
4 anchovy fillets, coarsely chopped
2 cloves garlic, coarsely chopped
Dash of hot sauce (such as Tabasco)
Dash of Worcestershire sauce
Kosher salt and freshly ground black pepper to taste
2 hearts romaine lettuce, halved lengthwise
2 firm avocados, halved and pitted, skin left on
2 cups (500 mL) cherry tomatoes
2 oz (60 g) wedge fresh Parmesan, shaved
1 Tbsp (15 mL) thinly sliced fresh basil

THE RAINFORD METHOD

1. Combine the oil, balsamic vinegar, mustard, lemon juice, anchovies, garlic, hot sauce,
   Worcestershire sauce, and salt and pepper to taste in a blender. Purée until smooth.
2. Fire up your charcoal or preheat your gas grill. You need a medium-high grilling temp
   of around 350°F (180°C). Prep the grill for cooking over direct heat.
3. Drizzle a small amount of the vinaigrette over the romaine lettuce in a large bowl.
   Place the lettuce on the grill, cut sides down. Grill for 30 seconds to 1 minute or until
   lightly charred. Remove from the grill, and place on a serving platter.
4. Toss the avocados and tomatoes with a small amount of the remaining vinaigrette in
   the same bowl. Place on the grill, arranging the avocados skin-side up. Cook for 1 to 2
   minutes or until warm and slightly softened.
5. Remove from the grill. Scatter the tomatoes over the lettuce. Scoop the avocado flesh
   out of the skin. Slice the avocado flesh and scatter over the lettuce.
6. Top the salad with Parmesan shavings. Drizzle with the remaining vinaigrette and
   sprinkle with basil.

Makes 8 servings

GAME BIRDS AND BARBECUE go hand in hand. While most people would choose chicken for their backyard barbecue, I'm always interested in grilling up birds like Cornish hens, quail and pheasant. Cornish hens, in particular, remind me of when my twin brother and I went on a road trip to New York City when we were 13 years old to visit our aunt. I'll always remember how she cooked these hens for us and how tasty they were.

Quail and pheasant, on the other hand, weren't something I'd taste until I was in my 20s. If you're tired of chicken and you dare to spice it up a touch, then this menu is for you. I've used a lot of cooking methods in my life and there's nothing like a rotisserie-grilled bird. But, that's not all that can be done on your grill. I've got some exciting side dishes to accompany the stars!

GAME TIME

Rotisserie Butter-and-Sage **CORNISH HEN**

Chinese **FIVE-SPICED QUAIL**

Tea-Smoked **BREAST OF PHEASANT**

GREEN PAPAYA SALAD

Green and Yellow **BEAN SALAD** *with Tangy Vinaigrette*

ROTISSERIE BUTTER-AND-SAGE CORNISH HEN

The vegetables impart a wonderful aromatic flavor to the Cornish hens, so don't feel guilty about throwing them away before serving—they've done their job.

2 lemons

2 large onions, coarsely chopped

2 ribs celery, coarsely chopped

1 large carrot, coarsely chopped

½ fennel bulb, coarsely chopped

2 cloves garlic, coarsely chopped

8 Cornish game hens

6 Tbsp (90 mL) unsalted butter, softened

½ tsp (2 mL) hot sauce

½ tsp (2 mL) Worcestershire sauce

Kosher salt and freshly ground black pepper to taste

16 whole fresh sage leaves

3 Tbsp (45 mL) olive oil (approx.)

THE RAINFORD METHOD

1. Fire up your charcoal or preheat your gas grill and prep the grill for using the rotisserie. Grilling temp should be around 325°F (160°C). For charcoal grilling, you're ready to grill when a thick white ash has appeared on the coals. Move most of the hot coals to the middle of the grill and place a few on either side to create heat in the middle of the grill where the Cornish hens will be rotating.

2. Finely grate 1 tsp (5 mL) zest from one of the lemons. Set aside.

3. Cut both lemons in half. Toss together the lemon halves, onions, celery, carrot, fennel, and garlic. Loosely stuff an equal portion of the vegetable mixture into the cavity of each hen.

4. Blend the butter with the reserved lemon zest, hot sauce, Worcestershire sauce, and salt and pepper to taste until well combined.

▶

5. Carefully lift the skin of the breasts of each Cornish hen and insert a sage leaf on each side of the breast.

6. Brush the Cornish hens with olive oil and rub the butter mixture evenly over the skin. Tie the wings behind each hen and tie its legs together to prevent the vegetables from falling out of the cavities.

7. Position one of the rotisserie forks at one end of the rotisserie rod. Slide the hens onto the rod and secure the remaining fork. Place a drip pan directly on the grates in the middle section of the grill. This will help to catch any fats that drip from the Cornish hens during cooking.

8. Put the rotisserie rod on the grill, making sure the rod is secure. Close the lid, set the motor speed to low, then let your grill do the rest of the work. Cook for 1 ½ to 2 hours or until the internal temperature of the Cornish hens reaches 170°F (76°C).

9. Remove the Cornish hens from the rotisserie and let stand for 10 to 15 minutes before serving them.

Makes 8 servings

CHINESE FIVE-SPICED QUAIL

This recipe is sure to be a big hit at your next dinner party.

Quail

4 cloves garlic, finely chopped
1 Tbsp (15 mL) Chinese five-spice powder
1 Tbsp (15 mL) sesame oil
1 Tbsp (15 mL) grapeseed oil
1 tsp (5 mL) finely grated fresh ginger
Kosher salt and freshly ground
        black pepper to taste
8 quail, each about 4 to 5 oz (125 to 150 g)
Canola oil for greasing

Sauce

⅓ cup (80 mL) orange juice
⅓ cup (80 mL) Beck's beer
3 Tbsp (45 mL) hoisin sauce
3 Tbsp (45 mL) ketchup
1 Tbsp (15 mL) chili sauce
⅓ green onion, coarsely chopped
1 clove garlic, finely grated
½ tsp (2 mL) finely grated fresh ginger
⅓ cup (80 mL) liquid honey

THE RAINFORD METHOD

1. For the quail, blend together the garlic, five-spice powder, sesame oil, grapeseed oil, ginger, and salt and pepper to taste. Set aside.
2. Cut the back bone out of each quail and remove bones from the chest, leg and wings. (Or have your butcher de-bone the quail.)
3. Toss the quail with the spice mixture in a large bowl. Refrigerate for at least 20 minutes or up to 1 hour.
4. Meanwhile, make the sauce by stirring together the orange juice, beer, hoisin sauce, ketchup, chili sauce, green onion, garlic and ginger in a small saucepan set over medium heat. Bring to a boil, then simmer until slightly thickened. Stir in the honey until well combined. Remove from the heat.
5. Fire up your charcoal grill and prep the grill for cooking over indirect heat. You need a medium-high temperature of around 350°F (180°C) to grill the quail. For gas grills, preheat the grill to medium-high then turn off one burner to achieve indirect heat. Oil the grate with canola oil.
6. Place the quail on the hot side of the grill and sear them for 2 minutes. Give each quail a quarter turn (from the 12 o' clock position to the 3 o'clock position) and cook for 2 minutes or until the skin is golden brown.
7. Flip the quail over and move them to the cooler part of the grill. Cook for 3 to 5 minutes for medium-rare, or to desired doneness. Brush the quail with the honey mixture during the last few minutes of grilling.
8. Take the quail off the grill and let stand for 5 minutes before serving.

Makes 4 servings for a main dish; 8 as an appetizer

TEA-SMOKED BREAST OF PHEASANT

Pheasant

4 Tbsp (60 mL) packed light brown sugar

4 Tbsp (60 mL) Chinese wine
(such as Shaoxing)

2 Tbsp (30 mL) finely grated fresh ginger

2 stalk fresh lemongrass, finely chopped
(about 4 Tbsp/60 mL)

1 ½ tsp (7 mL) Szechuan peppercorns

8 pheasant breasts, skin on

6 cups (1.5 L) apple wood chips,
soaked in water for at least 2 hours

2 cups (500 mL) dry apple wood chips

1 cup (250 mL) Chinese black tea leaves

Sauce

1 cup (250 mL) brewed black tea

6 Tbsp (90 mL) light soy sauce

6 Tbsp (90 mL) hoisin sauce

6 Tbsp (90 mL) liquid honey

4 Tbsp (60 mL) rice wine vinegar

2 Tbsp (30 mL) sesame oil

THE RAINFORD METHOD

1. For the pheasant, mix together the sugar, wine, ginger, lemongrass and peppercorns in a large bowl. Add the pheasant breasts and turn to coat. Cover and marinate in the fridge for 24 hours.

2. Combine two handfuls of wet apple wood chips with one handful of dry wood chips and half of the black tea leaves on a piece of foil. Fold the foil to fully enclose the mixture, sealing well. Poke several vent holes in the foil. When the first pouch burns out after about 1 hour, repeat with the remaining wood chips and tea to make a second pouch.

3. For the sauce, stir together the brewed tea, soy sauce, hoisin, honey, vinegar and sesame seed oil until combined. Set aside.

4. Fire up your charcoal grill and prep the grill for cooking over indirect heat. You need a medium-high temperature of around 350°F (180°C) to grill the pheasant. For gas grills, preheat the grill to medium-high then turn off one burner to achieve indirect heat.

5. Place one of the pouches of wood chips directly on top of the lit coals of a charcoal grill, or directly on the heated side of a gas grill.

6. When the chips begin to smoke, place the pheasant breasts over the wood chip pouch. Close the lid.

7. Cook for 2 minutes per side. Move the pheasant breasts to the cooler part of the grill and cook, basting with the tea mixture, for 20 to 30 minutes or until the internal temperature reaches 170°F (76°C).

8. Remove the pheasant breasts from the grill and let rest for 5 to 10 minutes before serving.

Makes 8 servings

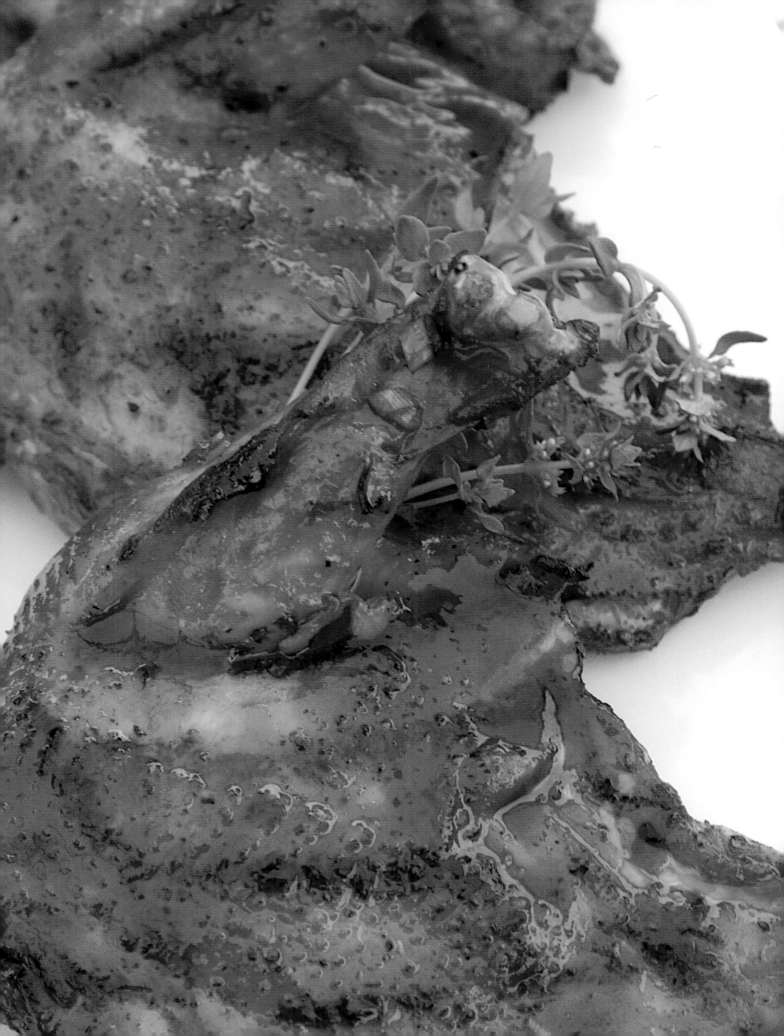

GREEN PAPAYA SALAD

This salad is delicious served cold or at room temperature.

2 cups (500 mL) peeled, seeded and shredded green papaya

½ cup (125 mL) julienned green beans

½ cup (125 mL) julienned carrot

½ cup (125 mL) alfalfa sprouts

⅓ cup (80 mL) fresh flat leaf parsley or coriander, coarsely chopped

2 Tbsp (30 mL) fresh lemon juice

3 cloves garlic, minced

2 Thai chilies, minced

2 tsp (10 mL) fish sauce

1 tsp (5 mL) packed brown sugar

Kosher salt and freshly ground black pepper to taste

THE RAINFORD METHOD

1. Toss together the papaya, green beans, carrot, alfalfa sprouts and parsley in a large salad bowl.
2. Whisk together the lemon juice, garlic, chilies, fish sauce and brown sugar until well combined and the sugar has dissolved.
3. Pour the dressing over the salad and toss well. Season with salt and pepper to taste. Place in the refrigerator until ready to serve, to give the flavors time to meld together.

Makes 8 servings

 **Tip:** *Use a mandoline slicer or a box grater to shred the papaya and carrot.*

GREEN and YELLOW BEAN SALAD with TANGY ViNAiGRETTE

¾ lb (375 g) green beans, trimmed

¾ lb (375 g) yellow beans, trimmed

Kosher salt to taste

3 Tbsp (45 mL) olive oil

2 tsp (10 mL) balsamic vinegar

2 tsp (10 mL) red wine vinegar

1 tsp (5 mL) Dijon mustard

Freshly ground black pepper to taste

2 large bunches of salad greens, such as frisée, washed and dried

6 green onions, thinly sliced

3 Tbsp (45 mL) finely chopped fresh oregano

THE RAINFORD METHOD

1. Place the beans in a large pot of well-salted, boiling water for 3–4 minutes or until tender-crisp. Reserve ¼ cup (60 mL) of the blanching water, then drain the beans and immediately plunge them into ice water.

2. Whisk together the reserved blanching water, olive oil, balsamic vinegar, red wine vinegar, mustard, and pepper to taste until well combined.

3. Arrange the salad greens on a large platter. Place the cooked beans on top. Drizzle with the vinaigrette and sprinkle with green onions and oregano. Serve within 1 hour of dressing.

Makes 8 servings

Tip: *Plunging green vegetables, such as beans, asparagus or broccoli, into an ice bath after blanching stops the cooking process and allows the vegetable to maintain its bright color.*

SOME DAYS YOU JUST SIT and stare at the barbecue and you say to yourself what else can I cook on the grill? Well, with this menu, you've caught me in one of those "what else" moments.

Although most people only cook turkey at Thanksgiving and Christmas, my rolled turkey recipe will have you thinking about it all year round, like I do. To go with the turkey roll, is grilled citrus and herb chicken, which is based on a tried-and-true recipe my family loves.

I've also included a few recipes I've been working on over the years for my vegetarian brothers and sisters: Grilled Asparagus Quiche, Portobello Mushroom Napoleons and a very nice smoked beet carpaccio. As a carnivore, I adore meat but making sure that there's something on the menu for everyone is important to me.

FROM QUICHE TO TURKEY, ALL ON THE GRILL

Grilled **CITRUS AND HERB CHICKEN**

Grilled **ROLLED TURKEY LEGS**

Grilled **ASPARAGUS QUICHE**

PORTOBELLO MUSHROOM Napoleons

SMOKED BEET CARPACCIO with Arugula Salad

GRILLED CITRUS and HERB CHICKEN

½ cup (125 mL) olive oil

2 Tbsp (30 mL) finely grated lemon zest

4 Tbsp (60 mL) fresh lemon juice

2 Tbsp (30 mL) finely grated orange zest

4 Tbsp (60 mL) fresh orange juice

2 Tbsp (30 mL) finely chopped fresh rosemary

2 Tbsp (30 mL) finely chopped fresh thyme

4 cloves garlic, finely grated

2 chickens, each about 4 lb (1.8 kg), cut in half through the breast and backbone

Kosher salt and freshly ground black pepper to taste

2 Tbsp (30 mL) finely chopped parsley

½ tsp (2 mL) dried red chili flakes

THE RAINFORD METHOD

1. Whisk together the oil, lemon zest and juice, orange zest and juice, rosemary and thyme until well combined. Reserve half of the mixture for the following day.

2. Place remaining citrus mixture, chicken and garlic in a very large resealable plastic bag. Give it a good massage through the bag and marinate in the fridge overnight.

3. Fire up your charcoal grill and prep the grill for cooking over indirect heat. You need a medium-high temperature of around 350°F (180°C) to grill the chicken. For gas grills, preheat the grill to medium-high then turn off one burner to achieve indirect heat.

4. Remove the chicken from the marinade, discarding the used marinade. Season the chicken with salt and pepper to taste.

5. Sear the chicken halves by placing them skin-side down on the hot side of the grill. Cook for 5 to 6 minutes. Turn each half through a quarter turn (from the 12 o'clock position to 3 o'clock). Cook for 5 to 6 minutes or until the skin is golden brown.

6. Flip each half over and move to the cooler side of the grill. Cook for 40 to 45 minutes or until the internal temperature reaches 170°F (76°C) and the juices run clear. Baste the chicken during the last 5 minutes of cooking with the reserved citrus mixture.

7. Remove the chicken halves from the grill and let rest for 5 to 10 minutes before carving.

Makes 8 servings

 Tip: *Use an instant-read thermometer to test for doneness by inserting it in the thickest part of the thigh but not touching the bone. The legs and thighs always take the longest to cook.*

GRiLLED ROLLED TURKEY LEGS

4 turkey legs, deboned (*see sidebar*)
2 slices white bread, crusts removed
¼ cup (60 mL) milk
8 oz (250 g) ground veal
2 shallots, finely chopped
2 cloves garlic, minced
2 Tbsp (30 mL) Cognac
1 Tbsp (15 mL) finely chopped fresh parsley
1 Tbsp (15 mL) olive oil
1 egg yolk
Kosher salt and freshly ground
         black pepper to taste

THE RAINFORD METHOD

1. Lay a sheet of plastic wrap out on a clean work surface, top with a turkey leg and a second sheet of plastic wrap. Pound the turkey with a kitchen mallet or heavy-bottom pot until the surface area is 25 to 35% larger than its original size. Repeat with the remaining turkey legs.

2. Place the bread in a shallow dish and pour over the milk. Let soak until the bread can be mashed into a paste.

3. Gently mix together the veal, shallots, garlic, Cognac, parsley and olive oil. Add the bread paste, egg yolk and salt and pepper to taste.

4. For each turkey leg, cut six to eight 6-inch (15 cm) lengths of butcher's twine. Lay the pieces of butcher's twine 2 inches (5 cm) apart on a cutting board.

5. Lay a turkey leg over the butcher's twine. Season with salt and pepper. Spread one-quarter of the stuffing evenly over the turkey leg and roll into a cylinder. Secure the turkey leg by tying the twine around it, trimming any excess twine. Repeat with remaining legs. Refrigerate until the grill is heated.

6. Fire up your charcoal grill and prep the grill for cooking over indirect heat. You need a medium-high temperature of around 350°F (180°C) to grill the turkey. For gas grills, preheat the grill to medium-high then turn off one burner to achieve indirect heat.

7. Sear the turkey legs by placing them on the hot side of the grill. Cook for 5 minutes per side or until well marked. Move the turkey legs to the cooler part of the grill. Close the lid and cook for 20 to 30 minutes or until the internal temperature reaches 170°F (76°C).

8. Remove from the grill and let rest for 10 minutes before carving.

Makes 8 servings

HOW TO DEBONE A TURKEY LEG

1. Lay turkey leg, skin side down, on a clean cutting board.

2. Using a very sharp boning knife, start at the bottom of the leg and run it gently along the center of the leg, following the bone up to the thigh.

3. Ease your knife under the bone. This will loosen it, and with a little finesse, the bone will come right out.

4. After the bone is out, remove any grizzle or tendons that are left behind.

5. When all else fails, have your butcher do it for you!

GRiLLED ASPARAGUS QUiCHE

They say real men don't eat quiche but, if you make it on the grill, guess what they'll be eating and loving? I like to use my grill for things that are usually made in the oven because it allows me to stay outside and that, my friends, is what I call awesome.

1 lb (500 g) pencil-thin asparagus, trimmed

4 Tbsp (60 mL) olive oil

Kosher salt and freshly ground black pepper to taste

1 unbaked 9-inch (23 cm) pie shell

(see dough recipe on page 157 or buy one ready made)

2 cups (500 mL) 18% table cream

4 eggs

¼ tsp (1 mL) freshly ground white pepper

⅛ tsp (0.5 mL) ground nutmeg

1 cup (250 mL) shredded Swiss cheese

½ cup (125 mL) shredded aged white cheddar

THE RAINFORD METHOD

1. Fire up your charcoal grill and prep the grill for cooking over indirect heat. You need a medium-high temperature of around 350°F (180°C) to grill the asparagus. For gas grills, preheat the grill to medium-high then turn off one burner to achieve indirect heat.

2. Toss the asparagus with the oil, salt and pepper. Grill over direct heat for 1 minute or until lightly marked. Cool completely.

3. Leave the grill on or preheat the oven to 350°F (180°C). Fill the pie crust with weights and bake it blind on the grill or in the oven for 10 minutes or until the dough is lightly golden around the edges but still raw in the center. Let cool slightly.

4. Whisk together the cream, eggs, white pepper, nutmeg and salt to taste. Sprinkle the Swiss and cheddar cheeses over the bottom of the pie shell. Pour the egg mixture over the cheese and top with the grilled asparagus.

5. Place the quiche on the grill over indirect heat. Close the lid. Cook for 40 minutes or until the crust is golden and filling is set. Or bake in the oven for the same amount of time. Allow to rest for 10 minutes before slicing.

Makes 6 to 8 servings

QUICHE DOUGH

1 cup (250 mL) all-purpose flour
¼ cup (60 mL) cold vegetable shortening, cubed
½ tsp (2 mL) kosher salt
¼ cup (60 mL) ice water

THE RAINFORD METHOD

1. Mix the flour, shortening and salt using a fork to combine the ingredients until crumbly. Stir in the water using the fork. Form the dough into a ball. Chill the dough in the refrigerator for 30 minutes or the freezer for 15 minutes.
2. Roll the dough out on a lightly floured surface to fit a 9-inch (23 cm) metal or foil pie plate or tart pan. Line the plate with the pastry and trim the edges. Poke several holes in the base of the pastry with a fork. Place a piece of parchment paper, the size of the pie plate, over the dough and top with dried beans. Bake as directed in Grilled Asparagus Quiche recipe (page 154).

Makes one 9-inch (23 cm) pie crust

PORTOBELLO MUSHROOM NAPOLEONS

Every time I use my limited vegetarian brain, I get so excited. As a meat eater I have to remind myself that some of the guests coming to my backyard need special attention. This recipe is a nice step in that direction.

3 sheets frozen puff pastry dough,
      thawed for 10 minutes

1 egg, beaten

3 Tbsp (45 mL) white sesame seeds

1 lb (500 g) ripe beefsteak tomatoes

1 medium red onion

¼ cup (60 mL) extra virgin olive oil, divided

Kosher salt and freshly ground
      black pepper to taste

2 Tbsp (30 mL) balsamic vinegar

2 garlic cloves, finely grated

16 medium Portobello mushroom caps

Special Sauce

1 cup (250 mL) mayonnaise

2 Tbsp (30 mL) prepared basil pesto

1 green onion, sliced

Dash of hot sauce

2 cups (500 mL) baby spinach, shredded

16 slices fontina cheese

THE RAINFORD METHOD

1. Fire up your charcoal grill and prep the grill for cooking over indirect heat. You need a medium-high temperature of around 350°F (180°C). For gas grills, preheat the grill to medium-high then turn off one burner to achieve indirect heat.

2. Roll out each sheet of puff pastry on a lightly floured surface to ⅛ inch (3 mm) thickness. Using a 3-inch (8 cm) metal cookie cutter, cut each sheet of dough into 8 rounds.

3. Place the 24 rounds on a parchment-paper-lined baking sheet. Brush rounds lightly with egg and sprinkle 8 of the rounds with the sesame seeds. Chill for 15 minutes.

4. Place the baking sheet on the grill over indirect heat and close the lid. Bake for 12 to 14 minutes or until golden brown. Remove from the grill and cool completely.

5. Meanwhile, use a mandoline slicer or very sharp knife to slice the tomatoes and onion into ¼-inch (6 mm) thick rounds. Place the tomato and onion slices on a baking sheet, brush lightly with 2 Tbsp (30 mL) oil and season with salt and pepper to taste.

6. Place the baking sheet on the grill over direct heat. Grill the tomatoes and onions for 2 to 3 minutes or until soft and nicely charred. Remove and set aside.

▶

7. Whisk together the remaining oil, balsamic vinegar and garlic in a large bowl. Add the mushroom caps and toss well. Season with salt and pepper to taste. Place the mushrooms on the grill and cook for 10 to 12 minutes or until nicely charred. Remove and set aside.

8. Meanwhile make the special sauce by stirring together the mayonnaise, pesto, green onion and hot sauce until well combined.

9. To assemble the napoleons, lay out 8 plain puff pastry rounds. Top each with a little special sauce, some shredded spinach, a mushroom cap, an onion slice and a slice of cheese.

10. Add a second plain puff pastry round to each stack, then layer with additional special sauce, another mushroom cap, another slice of cheese and a tomato slice. Cap each stack with a sesame seed puff pastry round.

11. Carefully transfer the napoleons to a baking sheet and place on the grill over indirect heat. Close the lid and cook for 5 to 7 minutes or until the cheese just begins to melt. Serve immediately.

Makes 8 servings

 Tip: For a better presentation, try to match the diameter of the mushrooms, tomatoes and onion.

SMOKED BEET CARPACCIO with ARUGULA SALAD

6 medium beets, trimmed
1 cup (250 mL) olive oil, divided
1 cup (250 mL) red wine vinegar, divided
½ tsp (2 mL) liquid honey
2 cups (500 mL) apple wood chips, soaked in water for at least 2 hours
4 cups (1 L) lightly packed arugula
1 Tbsp (15 mL) very thinly sliced fresh basil

THE RAINFORD METHOD

1. Place the unpeeled beets in a saucepan and cover with cold water. Bring to a boil and cook for 12 to 15 minutes or until tender. Drain and remove the skins.
2. Meanwhile, whisk together ½ cup (125 mL) oil, ½ cup (125 mL) red wine vinegar and honey until combined.
3. Place beets and oil mixture in a resealable plastic bag. Refrigerate for 24 hours.
4. Fire up your charcoal grill and prep the grill for cooking over indirect heat. You need a low temperature of around 250°F (120°C). For gas grills, preheat the grill to low then turn off one burner to achieve indirect heat.
5. For charcoal grills, place apple wood chips directly on top of the hot coals. For gas barbecues, place the wood chips in a foil pouch and place the pouch directly on the heated side of the grill.
6. Place the beets over indirect heat. Close the lid and cook for 15 to 20 minutes or until just warm. Remove from the grill and let cool to room temperature. Place beets in the refrigerator or until chilled.
7. Cut the beets into ⅛-inch (3 mm) slices. Even up the slices using a round cookie cutter. Whisk the remaining oil with the remaining vinegar and toss with the arugula to coat (you can store any leftover dressing in the fridge for other salads). Pile arugula on a serving platter. Sprinkle with basil and surround with the beets.

Makes 6 to 8 servings

Tip: *Wear rubber gloves when peeling the beets.*
Beets are easier to slice when they're cold, so don't skip the chilling step.
Use a mandoline slicer to slice the beets very thinly.

EVEN AS A CHEF, I know how hard it can be to cook fish well on the barbecue. But, cooking fish on the barbecue is one of the things that everyone should feel comfortable about. The first step is picking the right fish. The problem most people have is with fish sticking to the grill. Swordfish and monkfish are ideal for the barbecue because they have dense flesh which isn't prone to sticking.

Mackerel is a delicate fish and its skin can tear easily so I suggest using a fish basket for this recipe to eliminate the tension-filled flip. Since fish is such a light protein, I serve it, here, with a hearty artichoke side, and a romaine heart salad.

FRESH FISH, ANYONE?

Grilled **SWORDFISH** with **PUTTANESCA RELISH**

MONKFISH TAILS IN BACON with Grilled Ratatouille

West Indian **GRILLED MACKEREL**

Grilled **ARTICHOKES** with Classic Beurre Blanc

Garden Green **ROMAINE HEARTS** with Anchovy Crostini

GRiLLED SWORDFiSH
with PUTTANESCA RELiSH

Puttanesca is a classic Italian mixture of tomatoes, capers and olives that is delicious with swordfish but goes equally well with sushi-grade tuna steaks.

Swordfish
¼ cup (60 mL) olive oil
1 lemon, zested and juiced
2 cloves garlic, crushed
8 fresh basil leaves, coarsely chopped
6 swordfish steaks,
     each about 7 oz (200 g)
Kosher salt and freshly ground
     black pepper to taste

Puttanesca Relish
2 cups (500 mL) cherry tomatoes, halved
¾ cup (185 mL) black olives,
     pitted and coarsely chopped
½ cup (125 mL) olive oil
2 shallots, finely diced
3 Tbsp (45 mL) drained baby capers, rinsed
3 cloves garlic, grated
4 anchovy fillets, chopped
1 Tbsp (15 mL) finely chopped fresh oregano
1 Tbsp (15 mL) fresh lemon juice
1 small red chili, seeded and diced

THE RAINFORD METHOD

1. Whisk together the oil, lemon zest and juice, garlic and basil in a shallow dish. Add the swordfish in a single layer. Marinate, turning once halfway through, for 2 hours in the fridge.

2. For the puttanesca relish, stir together the tomatoes, olives, olive oil, shallots, capers, garlic, anchovies, oregano, lemon juice and chili. Let stand for at least 1 hour at room temperature before serving.

3. Fire up your charcoal or preheat your gas grill. You need a medium-high grilling temp of around 350°F (180°C). Prep the grill for cooking over direct heat.

4. Remove the swordfish from the marinade. Season with salt and pepper. Place the swordfish on the grill and cook for 3 minutes or until well marked. Rotate the steaks a quarter turn (from 12 o'clock to 3 o'clock). Cook for 3 minutes or until well marked. Flip the steaks over and continue to cook for an additional 4 minutes or until the flesh is opaque.

5. Serve the fish topped with puttanesca relish.

Makes 6 servings

MONKFISH TAILS IN BACON
with GRILLED RATATOUILLE

Monkfish anyone? Well, if you add bacon and some veg you've just hit a grand-slam home run. Some of you might have heard monkfish described as the poor man's lobster and it's true. This is one meaty, tasty fish.

2 lb (1 kg) monkfish tails
Kosher salt and freshly ground black pepper to taste
16 slices bacon
1 large sweet red pepper, seeded and quartered
1 large sweet yellow pepper, seeded and quartered
1 red onion, thickly sliced
4 ripe plum tomatoes, cored and halved
1 large zucchini, cut into quarters lengthwise
1 small eggplant, cut into quarters crosswise
¼ cup (60 mL) olive oil
1 large head garlic, roasted
Good-quality extra virgin olive oil for drizzling
8 large fresh basil leaves, coarsely shredded

THE RAINFORD METHOD

1. Rub a knife between the membrane and the meat of the monkfish tails. Pull the membrane off and cut out any pieces that are left behind.
2. Cut each monkfish tail into two 8 oz (250 g) pieces. Season the monkfish with salt and pepper, then wrap each piece in 4 bacon slices. Chill in the fridge.
3. Fire up your charcoal or preheat your gas grill. You need a medium-high grilling temp of around 350°F (180°C). Prep the grill for cooking over direct heat.
4. Toss together the red pepper, yellow pepper, onion, tomatoes, zucchini, eggplant, oil, and salt and pepper to taste. Place the vegetables on the grill and cook for 5 minutes.
5. Add the monkfish to the grill alongside the vegetables. Cook the monkfish, turning as needed, for 4 to 5 minutes or until the fish is just firm and the bacon is crisp.
6. Arrange the vegetables on a platter (alternating the types of vegetable for a great presentation) and top with the roasted garlic cloves. Place the grilled monkfish on top. Drizzle with extra virgin olive oil and sprinkle with basil.

Makes 4 servings

WEST INDIAN GRILLED MACKEREL

When I was a kid, my mom used to fix mackerel all the time. This recipe is me making up to her for all those times I complained about the smell in the house afterward. This is for you, Mom!

¼ cup (60 mL) dry breadcrumbs
2 Tbsp (30 mL) finely chopped fresh thyme
2 Tbsp (30 mL) coarsely chopped fresh parsley
1 tsp (5 mL) finely grated lemon zest
½ tsp (2 mL) finely chopped fresh dill
Kosher salt and freshly ground black pepper to taste
8 whole mackerel (heads on), about 3 ½ lb (1.75 kg)
6 Tbsp (90 mL) olive oil

THE RAINFORD METHOD

1. Fire up your charcoal or preheat your gas grill. You need a medium-high grilling temp of around 350°F (180°C). Prep the grill for cooking over direct heat.
2. Toss together the breadcrumbs, thyme, parsley, lemon zest, dill, and salt and pepper to taste.
3. Make slits on both sides of each mackerel. Rub herb mixture into the slits. Drizzle the fish with oil.
4. If you are cooking fish for the first time on the barbecue, use a fish basket to make the process less daunting. Otherwise, if you're used to grilling, place the fish on the grill. Cook for 5 to 6 minutes per side or until the fish flakes easily.

Makes 8 servings

Tip: *To prevent the mackerel from sticking, top the grate with a piece of aluminum foil before adding the fish.*

GRiLLED ARTiCHOKES
with CLASSiC BEURRE BLANC

If you like, add chopped fresh mint and a squeeze of lemon juice to the classic beurre blanc recipe for this artichoke dish.

2 lemons, halved
1 cup (250 mL) olive oil (approx.)
1 cup (250 mL) dry white wine
6 cloves garlic, thinly sliced
6 sprigs fresh thyme
1 Tbsp (15 mL) whole black peppercorns
Kosher salt to taste
6 large artichokes
Freshly ground black pepper to taste
Classic Beurre Blanc *(see recipe on page 175)*

THE RAINFORD METHOD

1. Place 6 cups (1.5 L) water in a large pot. Squeeze the lemons into the water. Add the lemon shells, oil, wine, garlic, thyme, peppercorns and salt to taste to the pot.
2. Remove and discard the tough outer leaves of the artichokes by pulling them toward the stem until the smaller, tender leaves are revealed. Cut about 1 inch (2.5 cm) off the top of each artichoke. Using a paring knife, trim the dark green part from the bottom of each artichoke, leaving the stem intact. Peel the stems. Cut the artichokes in half lengthwise and remove the fuzz and purple leaves from the hearts of the artichokes.
3. Submerge the artichokes halves in the pot of lemon water, adding more water if necessary. Put a plate or small lid directly on top of the artichokes so that they stay submerged.
4. Bring to a boil over medium-high heat. Cook, covered, for 10 minutes or until just tender. Drain well and cool completely.
5. Fire up your charcoal or preheat your gas grill. You need a medium-high grilling temp of around 350°F (180°C). Prep the grill for cooking over direct heat.
6. Brush the artichokes with a little olive oil and season with salt and pepper to taste. Place the artichokes cut-sides down on the grill. Cook, turning once, for 7 to 10 minutes or until well marked.
7. Place the artichokes on a platter and spoon beurre blanc *(see recipe on page 175)* over the top.

Makes 12 servings

 Tip: *Artichokes discolor quite fast when cut. To prevent this, rub any exposed areas of the artichoke with a cut lemon as you go.*

CLASSIC BEURRE BLANC

½ cup (125 mL) dry white wine
1 ½ Tbsp (22.5 mL) white wine vinegar
1 Tbsp (15 mL) chopped shallots
½ lb (250 g) unsalted butter, cut into small pieces
Kosher salt

THE RAINFORD METHOD

1. Combine the wine, vinegar and shallots in a saucepan. Simmer until the liquid has reduced to about 1 Tbsp (15 mL). Gradually add the butter to the hot reduction, whisking vigorously.
2. When the butter is incorporated and nearly melted, remove the saucepan from the heat and continue to whisk until the sauce is smooth. Strain the sauce and season with salt.

Makes about 1 cup (250 mL)

GARDEN GREEN ROMAiNE HEARTS
with ANCHOVY CROSTiNi

8 slices pancetta

8 oil-packed anchovy fillets, drained

2 Tbsp (30 mL) olive oil (approx.)

16 slices baguette (sliced diagonally)

2 egg yolks

¾ cup (185 mL) grapeseed oil

2 Tbsp (30 mL) Moutarde de Meaux (French grain mustard)

2 Tbsp (30 mL) red wine vinegar

1 clove garlic, minced

1 tsp (5 mL) 35% whipping cream

½ tsp (2 mL) liquid honey

Kosher salt and freshly cracked white pepper to taste

4 romaine lettuce hearts

2 cups (500 mL) shaved Parmesan cheese

THE RAINFORD METHOD

1. Fire up your charcoal grill and prep the grill for cooking over indirect heat. You need a medium-high temperature of 350 to 400°F (180 to 200°C). For gas grills, preheat the grill to medium-high then turn off one burner to achieve indirect heat.

2. Arrange the pancetta on a parchment-paper-lined baking sheet. Place the baking sheet over indirect heat. Cook for 15 to 20 minutes or until brown and crisp. Let cool.

3. Meanwhile, purée the anchovies by chopping them into small pieces, then using the flat side of a chef's knife to mash them into a smooth paste. Add 1 Tbsp (15 mL) olive oil to make the mixture spreadable.

4. Brush both sides of the baguette slices with some of the remaining olive oil. Grill over direct heat for 2 minutes per side or until lightly golden. Remove from the grill and brush each slice with anchovy paste. Set aside.

5. Whisk the egg yolks with the grape seed oil, mustard, red wine vinegar, garlic, cream, honey, and salt and pepper to taste until well combined.

6. Increase the grill temperature to high. Cut the romaine lettuce hearts in half lengthwise, leaving the root ends intact. Brush with the remaining olive oil. Grill, cut sides down, over direct heat for 30 seconds or until well marked.

7. Cut the romaine into bite-size pieces and toss with dressing in a large bowl. Divide the salad between eight plates and top each portion with a pancetta round and two anchovy crostini. Sprinkle with Parmesan.

Makes 8 servings

FISH IS THE ONE INGREDIENT that can make some people think twice about using the grill, but some of your favorite spices and wooden planks can make all the difference.

When it comes to creating recipes, my best time for inspiration is when I'm standing in the middle of a fish store where I can inspect the fish up close and choose what variety I'll buy. The salmon recipe in this menu is a winner and will have everyone at your party asking for more. I've accompanied it with a chermoula rub that has Algerian, Moroccan and Tunisian roots. It's also one of the first recipes I did on TV. The flavors are so well balanced, you'll be amazed.

Tuna is another fish I love using but it can be pricey so I've come up with a beautiful appetizer that teams a modest amount of tuna with pineapple and bacon. The last fish I use for this menu are fresh grilled sardines, a favorite of both my parents and in-laws.

FROM THE WEST COAST OF CANADA TO GREECE AND EVERYTHING IN BETWEEN

15

TUNA, PINEAPPLE and BACON SKEWERS with Sweet-and-Sour Sauce

Planked CHERMOULA-RUBBED SALMON

Classic GREEK GRILLED SARDINES

Summer's Best MIXED VEGETABLE GRILL

Lemon-and-Herb GRILLED ONION RINGS

TUNA, PiNEAPPLE and BACON SKEWERS with SWEET-AND-SOUR SAUCE

Here I've combined three foods I crave from time to time: tuna, pineapple and bacon. I really enjoy putting my favorite things on sticks; it makes them easier to serve and life that much more simple.

2 cups (500 mL) granulated sugar

¼ cup (60 mL) water

2 cups (500 mL) rice wine vinegar

2 Tbsp (30 mL) finely grated garlic

1 Tbsp (15 mL) finely grated fresh ginger

½ sweet red pepper, seeded and finely diced

16 slices of bacon, halved

1 ½ lb (750 g) sushi-grade yellow fin tuna, cut into 1 1/2-inch (4 cm) cubes

1 small pineapple, peeled, cored and cut into 1 1/2-inch (4 cm) cubes

16 8-inch (20 cm) wooden skewers, soaked in cold water for 2 hours

THE RAINFORD METHOD

1. Combine the sugar and water in a small saucepan set over high heat. Cook for 4 minutes or until sugar dissolves and starts to turn a caramel color.

2. Carefully add the vinegar, garlic and ginger (the caramel may splatter) and bring back to a boil. Simmer for 3 minutes, then stir in the red pepper. Remove from the heat and let cool completely.

3. Place 1 slice of the bacon on the work surface. Top the bacon with a cube of tuna, then a cube of pineapple. Roll up the bacon to enclose the tuna and pineapple, trimming the bacon if necessary. Thread onto a skewer where the bacon overlaps, skewering the tuna and pineapple.

4. Repeat with the remaining ingredients and skewers. Refrigerate for 1 hour or until chilled.

5. Fire up your charcoal or preheat your gas grill. You need a medium-high grilling temp of around 350°F (180°C). Prep the grill for cooking over direct heat.

6. Place the skewers on the grill and cook for 2 minutes. Flip and continue cooking for 1 to 2 minutes or until evenly browned. Serve immediately with the sauce for dipping.

Makes 8 servings

PLANKED CHERMOULA-RUBBED SALMON

Chermoula is usually made with herbs, oil, lemon juice, pickled lemons, garlic, cumin and salt. It can also include onion, fresh coriander, ground chilies, black pepper or saffron. Here, as a coating for salmon, I've taken chermoula to the next level!

½ cup (125 mL) fresh lemon juice

⅓ cup (80 mL) finely chopped fresh cilantro

¼ cup (60 mL) olive oil

3 Tbsp (45 mL) smoked paprika

3 cloves garlic, minced

1 ½ tsp (7.5 mL) cayenne

½ tsp (2 mL) ground cumin

Kosher salt and freshly ground black pepper to taste

8 salmon fillets with skin, each 8 oz (250 g)

2 untreated maple planks, soaked in water for 2 hours

THE RAINFORD METHOD

1. Combine the lemon juice, cilantro, olive oil, paprika, garlic, cayenne, cumin, and salt and pepper to taste in a shallow dish. Add the salmon, turning to coat. Cover and refrigerate for 2 hours.

2. Fire up your charcoal grill and prep the grill for cooking over indirect heat. You need a medium-high temperature of around 350°F (180°C) to grill the salmon. For gas grills, preheat the grill to medium-high then turn off one burner to achieve indirect heat.

3. Place the soaked maple planks on the grill over direct heat until the planks become dry and start to crackle.

4. Position the planks over indirect heat. Place the salmon on the planks and close the lid. Cook for 10 to 15 minutes for medium-rare, or to desired doneness.

Makes 8 servings

CLASSIC GREEK GRiLLED SARDiNES

These go great served with the lemon-and-herb grilled onion rings on page 189.

24 fresh sardines (heads and tails left on), cleaned
3 Tbsp (45 mL) Greek olive oil
Kosher salt and freshly ground black pepper to taste
Canola oil for greasing

THE RAINFORD METHOD

1. Rinse the sardines under cold water and dry with paper towels. Gently toss the sardines with olive oil, and salt and pepper to taste.
2. Fire up your charcoal or preheat your gas grill. You need a medium grilling temp of around 325°F (160°C). Prep the grill for cooking over direct heat.
3. Grease the grate well to prevent the sardines from sticking. Place the sardines on the grill and cook for 4 minutes per side or until the skin is slightly charred and the flesh is white and flakes easily when tested.

Makes 8 servings

SUMMER'S BEST MIXED VEGETABLE GRILL

1 cup (250 mL) olive oil (approx.)

2 lemons, juiced

Kosher salt and freshly ground black pepper to taste

6 zucchini, thinly sliced

6 yellow sweet peppers, seeded and quartered

4 Japanese eggplants, thinly sliced

2 red onions, cut into wedges

2 white onions, cut into wedges

2 cups (500 mL) Smoked Red Grape Tomatoes *(see recipe on page 188)*

1 cup (250 mL) very thinly sliced fresh basil

THE RAINFORD METHOD

1. Fire up your charcoal grill and prep the grill for cooking over indirect heat.
   You need a medium-high temperature of around 350°F (180°C) to grill the vegetables.
   For gas grills, preheat the grill to medium-high then turn off one burner to achieve
   indirect heat.
2. Stir together the oil, lemon juice and salt and pepper to taste. Reserve half of
   this mixture.
3. Toss all the vegetables, except the tomatoes, with the remaining oil mixture in
   a large bowl.
4. Place the vegetables over direct heat. Cook, turning as needed, until well marked.
5. Move the vegetables to the cooler part of the grill and cook, turning occasionally,
   until tender.
6. Arrange the vegetables on a serving platter, add the tomatoes and drizzle with the
   reserved oil mixture. Sprinkle with basil.

Makes 8 servings

SMOKED RED GRAPE TOMATOES

These delicious little tomatoes make a great topping for pastas and pizzas. If you have any left over, mix them with a little extra virgin olive oil and seal them in an airtight container to store in the fridge.

2 lb (1 kg) red grape tomatoes
2 Tbsp (30 mL) olive oil
Kosher salt and freshly ground white pepper to taste
2 handfuls apple wood chips, soaked in water for 2 hours
1 handful dry apple wood chips (optional)

THE RAINFORD METHOD

1. Toss the tomatoes with the olive oil and salt and pepper to taste. Spread them out on a rimmed baking sheet.
2. Fire up your charcoal grill and prep the grill for cooking over indirect heat. You need a temperature of around 220°F (104°C) to smoke the tomatoes. For gas grills, preheat the grill to 220°F (104°C), then turn off one burner to achieve indirect heat.
3. Once the charcoal grill is heated, place the soaked wood chips on top of the lit charcoal. For gas barbecues, wrap the soaked chips in a foil pouch and place the pouch directly on the heated side of the grill.
4. When the wood chips start to smoke, place the baking sheet on the cooler side of the grill. Close the lid.
5. After 30 minutes, the smoke will die down. If you want significant smoke flavor, add the dry wood chips at this time, scattering them directly over the lit coals or wrapping them in a foil pouch if you're using a gas barbecue.
6. Smoke the tomatoes, with the lid down, for 1 ½ to 2 hours or until they start to shrivel slightly.

Makes about 4 cups (1 L)

LEMON-and-HERB GRILLED ONION RINGS

¼ cup (60 mL) olive oil

2 Tbsp (30 mL) red wine vinegar

2 Tbsp (30 mL) fresh lemon juice

2 Tbsp (30 mL) finely chopped fresh thyme

2 Tbsp (30 mL) finely chopped
      fresh rosemary

2 Tbsp (30 mL) finely chopped fresh parsley

1 Tbsp (15 mL) finely grated lemon zest

4 sweet onions, cut into 1/2-inch
      (1 cm) slices

4 red onions, cut into 1/2-inch (1 cm) slices

Kosher salt and freshly ground black pepper
      to taste

THE RAINFORD METHOD

1. Whisk together the oil, vinegar, lemon juice, thyme, rosemary, parsley and lemon zest until well combined

2. Spread the onions in a single layer on a baking sheet. Season with salt and pepper to taste. Drizzle the oil mixture evenly over the onions. Cover and marinate in the fridge for 2 to 4 hours.

3. Fire up your charcoal grill and prep the grill for cooking over indirect heat. You need a medium-high temperature of around 350°F (180°C) to grill the onions. For gas grills, preheat the grill to medium-high then turn off one burner to achieve indirect heat.

4. Place the onion slices over indirect heat. Cook for 2 to 3 minutes per side or until well marked and slightly softened.

5. Arrange onions slices on a serving platter and serve warm or at room temperature.

Makes 6 to 8 servings

COLD SMOKE IS ONE OF THE BEST ways to infuse smoke flavor into the flesh of fish. After making tuna and salmon tartare for years, I thought I'd alter the recipe by infusing a little smoke into it. One of the challenges was to add gentle smoke flavor while not cooking the fish. I found that placing an ice bath below the fish on the grill kept the temperature from getting too high.

I've also been planking salmon for many years and wanted to change it up a bit so I came up with two flavors I think work extremely well together—maple syrup and mustard. The taste is amazing!

Taking your barbecuing to the next level will depend on how enthusiastically you embrace these new techniques. There are many ways to barbecue, and this is just another fun step in your evolution!

(16) SMOKE AND THE BEAUTIFUL FISH IT LOVES

Cold-Smoked **TUNA TARTARE** *with Asian Seasonings*

CEDAR-PLANKED SALMON *with Maple-Mustard Glaze*

Fast and Easy **GRILLED TUNA STEAKS**

TASTE-OF-GREEK-TOWN SALAD

COLD-SMOKED TUNA TARTARE
with ASIAN SEASONINGS

This tartare can be served on sliced cucumbers garnished with diced avocado. Crispy wontons are another nice option.

1 handful dry cherry wood chips

8 oz (250 g) sushi-grade yellow fin tuna steak

¼ cup (60 mL) finely chopped chives

1 Tbsp (15 mL) fresh lemon juice

1 Tbsp (15 mL) unseasoned rice wine vinegar

2 tsp (10 mL) soy sauce

¼ tsp (1 mL) sesame oil

Kosher salt and freshly cracked white pepper to taste

Thinly sliced English cucumber

Peeled, pitted and diced avocado tossed with fresh lemon juice

Deep-fried wonton wrapper strips and whole chives for garnish (optional)

THE RAINFORD METHOD

1. To prepare the smoker for cold smoke, fire up the charcoal fire box by adding 10 to 15 pieces of lump charcoal, using a chimney starter to light the charcoal. When the charcoal is covered with thick white ash, place a drip tray of ice on the cooler side of the smoker. This will help to keep the temperature as low as possible. Place one handful of dry wood chips directly on the heated coals.

2. Put the whole tuna steak on the cooler side of the smoker and allow the tuna to smoke for 5 minutes. Remove the tuna and place in the fridge. Let cool completely.

3. Place the cold tuna on a cutting board and cut into very small cubes. Transfer the cubed tuna to a bowl and add the chives, lemon juice, vinegar, soy sauce, sesame oil, and salt and white pepper to taste. Toss gently until well combined, then adjust the seasonings to taste.

4. Place cucumber slices on a serving platter. Place a 1-inch (2.5 cm) round cookie cutter on 1 cucumber slice. Spoon a little of the tuna mixture into the cookie cutter, pressing the mixture down gently. Carefully remove the cookie cutter.

5. Place a ½-inch (1 cm) cookie cutter on top of the tuna layer and fill with a little of the avocado. Remove the cookie cutter and garnish with deep-fried wonton wrapper strips and whole chives. Repeat with the remaining cucumber slices, tuna and avocado.

Makes 8 servings

Tip: *For best results, smoke the tuna in a charcoal smoker, following the manufacturer's instructions. If you only have a gas grill you can still do this recipe but it works best in a smoker. Use indirect heat on a gas grill and add an ice cube to a drip tray to keep the temperature down.*

CEDAR-PLANKED SALMON with MAPLE-MUSTARD GLAZE

*I just love the ease of grilling on planks. Not only do they infuse flavor but they make cleanup easy.
I enjoy the taste of cedar with the maple-mustard glaze on the salmon. You'll be making this a lot.*

1 Tbsp (15 mL) maple syrup
1 Tbsp (15 mL) Dijon mustard
1 Tbsp (15 mL) fresh lemon juice
1 Tbsp (15 mL) unsalted butter, melted
2 lb (1 kg) side of salmon, skin on
Kosher salt and freshly ground black pepper to taste
1 untreated cedar plank, about 16 x 8 inches (40 x 20 cm),
    soaked in water for at least 2 hours

THE RAINFORD METHOD

1. Fire up your charcoal grill and prep the grill for cooking over indirect heat. You need a medium temperature of around 325°F (160°C) to grill the salmon. For gas grills, preheat the grill to medium then turn off one burner to achieve indirect heat.
2. Whisk together the maple syrup, mustard, lemon juice and butter. Set aside.
3. Place the salmon skin-side down on a large cutting board. Using clean, needle-nose pliers, remove any pin bones from the salmon. Brush the maple syrup mixture evenly over the salmon. Season with salt and pepper to taste.
4. Place the cedar plank on the grill over direct heat until the plank becomes dry and starts to crackle.
5. Center the salmon skin-side-down on the plank. Cook, covered, for 15 to 25 minutes or until lightly browned on the surface.
6. If the plank starts to burn, move it to the cooler part of the grill and extinguish the flames by spraying them with a little water. Add an extra 4 to 5 minutes to the cooking time if you have to move the plank.
7. Use tongs and a spatula to carefully remove the salmon and the plank from the grill.

Makes 6 servings

FAST and EASY GRiLLED TUNA STEAKS

Grilled tuna steaks are so popular, it's natural that I'd include this quick and easy recipe for all of you fish lovers. Just make sure to get sushi-grade tuna for the best results.

6 tuna steaks, each 6 oz (175 g) and about 1 inch (2.5 cm) thick
3 Tbsp (45 mL) olive oil
Kosher salt and freshly ground black pepper to taste

THE RAINFORD METHOD

1. Fire up your charcoal or preheat your gas grill. You need a medium grilling temp of around 325°F (160°C). Prep the grill for cooking over direct heat.
2. Brush the tuna steaks lightly with oil and season with salt and pepper to taste.
3. Place the tuna steaks on the grill and cook for 2 to 3 minutes per side for rare, 4 to 5 minutes per side for medium-rare, 6 to 7 minutes per side for well done.

Makes 6 servings

TASTE-OF-GREEK-TOWN SALAD

This recipe is my homage to all the Greek Towns in the world, especially the one on the Danforth in Toronto. My wife and kids love when we go out for Greek but they also enjoy when I make magic at home.

½ cup (125 mL) extra virgin olive oil

2 Tbsp (30 mL) red wine vinegar

6 drained capers, finely chopped

2 cloves garlic, finely grated

1 anchovy fillet, chopped

2 tsp (10 mL) dried oregano leaves

Freshly ground black pepper to taste

8 plum tomatoes, each cut into 6 pieces

1 English cucumber, peeled and cut into ½-inch (1 cm) slices

1 red onion, thinly sliced

6 oz (175 g) feta cheese, cubed

⅓ cup (80 mL) kalamata olives, pitted

1 Tbsp (15 mL) fresh oregano leaves

THE RAINFORD METHOD

1. Whisk together the oil, red wine vinegar, capers, garlic, anchovy, dried oregano, and pepper to taste. Set aside for 1 hour at room temperature to allow the flavors to marry.
2. Gently toss together the tomatoes, cucumber, red onion, feta cheese, olives and fresh oregano in a large serving bowl.
3. Pour the dressing over the salad and toss lightly to coat evenly.

Makes 8 servings

WHEN IT COMES TO FISH, it's always good to keep in mind that practice makes perfect, and this menu is a great refresher course. When I think back to the time before I embraced all things culinary, I remember how I felt standing over heat and fish. Sometimes it worked and sometimes it didn't. Now I know that getting your grill hot enough is the secret to great barbecued fish. Keep that in mind while you grill your way through this menu.

This lineup really has you exploring the grill. I've got you blackening salmon, planking halibut, grilling striped bass and even making paella on the 'cue. I hope you have as much fun grilling this menu as I had creating it.

FiSH 101–
CLASS iN SESSiON

17

BLACKENED SALMON *with Maple Glaze*

SPANISH PAELLA *with Grilled Seafood*

Maple-Planked GARLIC HALIBUT

Grilled STRIPED BASS

HEIRLOOM TOMATO SALAD

BLACKENED SALMON with MAPLE GLAZE

Salmon has to be one of the world's most popular fish. I added the maple syrup to give it that uniquely Canadian twist. Oh, Canada!

Glaze
½ cup (125 mL) maple syrup
3 Tbsp (45 mL) fresh lime juice
½ tsp (2 mL) chili powder
1 clove garlic, minced
Kosher salt to taste

Salmon
2 Tbsp (30 mL) paprika
1 tsp (5 mL) chili powder
1 clove garlic, minced
½ tsp (2 mL) kosher salt
½ tsp (2 mL) freshly ground black pepper
4 lb (1.8 kg) skin-on, boneless salmon,
      cut into eight 8 oz (250 g) portions
Canola oil for greasing

THE RAINFORD METHOD

1. Fire up your charcoal or preheat your gas grill. You need a medium-high grilling temp of around 350°F (180°C). Prep the grill for cooking over direct heat.
2. For the glaze, stir together the maple syrup, lime juice, chili powder, garlic, and salt to taste in a small saucepan. Simmer until thick enough to coat the back of a spoon. Set aside.
3. For the salmon, mix together the paprika, chili powder, garlic, salt and pepper. Sprinkle generously over both sides of the salmon fillets.
4. Brush the grill with canola oil. Place the salmon fillets, flesh-side down, on the grill. Cook, without moving them, for 2 to 3 minutes or until browned. Flip the salmon fillets and cook for 3 to 4 minutes or until the skin is crisp. (Reduce the heat as needed to prevent scorching on a charcoal grill by moving some of the coals around to create a lower grilling temperature, or by reducing the heat of one burner on a gas grill.)
5. Close the lid and cook for an additional 2 to 3 minutes or until the fish flakes with a fork. Brush the glaze over the salmon during the last few minutes of cooking. Remove the salmon from the grill and let stand for 2 to 3 minutes before enjoying.

Makes 8 servings

SPANiSH PAELLA with GRiLLED SEAFOOD

This crowd-pleaser is the recipe to cook when you have a lot of people coming over for a party. It's really fun when all you have to do is grill up some seafood and stir Arborio rice with stock.

8 cups (2 L) chicken stock
    (see Rainford's Staple Recipes, page xvi)
¼ cup (60 mL) olive oil, divided
6 ripe plum tomatoes, peeled,
    seeded and chopped
1 medium onion, finely chopped
1 medium leek (white and light green parts
    only), thinly sliced and washed
½ sweet red pepper, seeded and chopped
½ sweet green pepper, seeded and chopped
2 garlic cloves, crushed
½ tsp (2 mL) saffron threads
2 ½ cups (625 mL) arborio rice
1 cup (250 mL) beer (I use Alexander Keith's
    Premium White beer)

1 bay leaf
1 lb (500 g) fresh mussels,
    washed and de-bearded
4 boneless, skinless chicken breasts
Kosher salt and freshly ground
    black pepper to taste
8 oz (250 g) cleaned squid, cut into rings
8 oz (250 g) monkfish tail, membrane removed
    and cut into 2-inch (5 cm) pieces
8 oz (250 g) medium shrimp (16/20 count),
    peeled with tails left intact
2 shell-on lobster tails
1 tsp (5 mL) smoked paprika

THE RAINFORD METHOD

1. Heat the chicken stock in a medium saucepan. Keep warm over low heat.
2. Heat half of the oil in a 15-inch (38 cm) paella pan set over medium heat. Add the tomatoes, onion, leek, red and green pepper, garlic and saffron. Cook for 8 to 10 minutes or until the vegetables are soft.
3. Stir in the rice. Cook, stirring constantly, for 3 to 5 minutes or until the rice is translucent. Pour in beer and simmer until it has evaporated.
4. Pour 1 cup (250 mL) of the warm chicken stock mixture into the paella pan and add the bay leaf. Cook, stirring occasionally, until the liquid is almost completely absorbed.
5. Repeat step 4, adding 1 cup (250 mL) of the stock at a time, for 15 minutes or until the rice is tender. Add the mussels during the last 5 minutes of cooking, discarding any mussels that fail to open after 5 minutes.

▶

6. Meanwhile, fire up your charcoal or preheat your gas grill. You need a medium-high grilling temp of around 350°F (180°C). Prep the grill for cooking over direct heat.
7. In a separate bowl, toss the squid, monkfish, shrimp and lobster tails with the remaining oil, and salt and pepper to taste.
8. Place the chicken and seafood on the grill. Cook, turning as needed, until a meat thermometer inserted into thickest chicken breast registers 170°F (76°C), and the seafood is firm but not overcooked.
9. Shell the lobster tails and chop the meat. Chop the chicken. Gently fold the cooked seafood and chicken into the cooked rice with any remaining stock. Stir in the paprika, and salt and pepper to taste. Serve straight from the paella pan.

Makes 8 to 10 servings

MAPLE-PLANKED GARLIC HALIBUT

Halibut may be one of those fish that conjures up thoughts of fish and chips, but as I get older I'm looking for healthier choices. By using my trusty maple planks, I've made this a recipe with more flavor and fewer calories. Give it a try.

4 Tbsp (60 mL) packed brown sugar

2 Tbsp (30 mL) fresh cilantro leaves

2 Tbsp (30 mL) finely grated ginger

4 cilantro roots, washed and finely chopped

4 cloves garlic, finely grated

½ cup (125 mL) fish sauce

6 Tbsp (90 mL) Chinese cooking wine (such as Shaoxing)

6 Tbsp (90 mL) sesame oil

2 Tbsp (30 mL) liquid honey

2 tsp (10 mL) kosher salt

2 tsp (10 mL) freshly ground black pepper

8 halibut steaks, each about 7 oz (200 g)

4 untreated maple planks, soaked in water for at least 2 hours

THE RAINFORD METHOD

1. Place the sugar, cilantro leaves, ginger, cilantro roots and garlic in a mortar. Grind with the pestle until the mixture forms a paste. Add the fish sauce, cooking wine, sesame oil, honey, salt and pepper.

2. Measure out one-quarter of the cilantro mixture and set aside. Place the remaining mixture in a resealable plastic bag with the halibut. Refrigerate for 1 hour.

3. Fire up your charcoal or preheat your gas grill. You need a medium-high grilling temp of around 350°F (180°C). Prep the grill for cooking over direct heat.

4. Remove the fish from marinade and place fish on planks. Place the planks on the grill and close the lid. Cook, basting with the reserved cilantro mixture, for 5 to 6 minutes or until the fish flakes easily.

Makes 8 servings

GRiLLED STRiPED BASS

8 skin-on striped bass fillets, each about 8 oz (250 g)
¼ cup (60 mL) olive oil
½ tsp (2 mL) kosher salt
½ tsp (2 mL) freshly ground white pepper
½ tsp (2 mL) dried chili flakes
Canola oil for greasing

THE RAINFORD METHOD

1. Fire up your charcoal or preheat your gas grill. You need a medium grilling temp of around 325°F (160°C). Prep the grill for cooking over direct heat.
2. Make four slits in the skin of each fillet. Brush the fillets with olive oil and season with salt, white pepper and chili flakes.
3. Grease the grate well with canola oil and place the fish on the grill. Cook for 6 to 8 minutes per side or until the skin is crisp and the flesh is opaque.

Makes 8 servings

Tip: Instead of oiling the grill, you can place a piece of foil between the grate and the fish to prevent it from sticking. If sticking becomes an issue, reposition the fillets to a cooler area of the grill to finish cooking.

For a beautiful, simple entrée, serve the bass with a seasonal salad and a rice pilaf.

HEiRLOOM TOMATO SALAD

This is a simple but delicious salad that will reinvent itself every time you prepare it because of the different sizes and colors of heirloom tomatoes.

3 lb (1.5 kg) heirloom tomatoes, cut into 1/2-inch (1 cm) wedges

8 to 10 fresh basil leaves

Kosher salt and freshly ground black pepper to taste

¼ cup (60 mL) extra virgin olive oil

2 Tbsp (30 mL) aged balsamic vinegar

1 tsp (5 mL) white truffle oil

Crusty bread to serve

THE RAINFORD METHOD

1. Place the tomatoes in a large serving bowl. Tear the basil and scatter on top of the tomatoes. Season with salt and pepper to taste.
2. Whisk together the oil, vinegar and truffle oil. Drizzle the dressing over the tomatoes and toss gently.
3. Serve with crusty bread.

Makes 6 to 8 servings

I PUT THIS MENU TOGETHER to prove to myself that even if you think you can't put it on the grill, you can. Don't limit your culinary potential and grilling endeavors.

For years I've wanted to put foie gras on the grill but I thought it would be too decadent. Well, given enough time those thoughts came to fruition and I'm now ready to share the results with you. We also have Grilled Tuna Lollipops, Beer and Juniper Berry Salmon and Crab-Filled Potato Boats—all tasty and surprisingly simple to make. But, the show stopper that may very well rock your socks are my Cast Iron Skillet Biscuits!

DECADENCE
MEETS THE
GRILL

Grilled **TUNA LOLLIPOPS** with Wasabi Foam

FOIE GRAS with Dried Cranberry and Shallot Compote

Beer and Juniper Berry **SALMON ON A CEDAR PLANK**

Crab-Filled **POTATO BOATS**

Cast Iron Skillet **BISCUITS**

GRiLLED TUNA LOLLiPOPS with WASABi FOAM

2 Tbsp (30 mL) grapeseed oil

1 Tbsp (15 mL) sesame oil

2 bay leaves

2 lb (1 kg) sushi-grade tuna, cut into sixteen 2- x 1-inch (5 x 2.5 cm) pieces

16 metal skewers, or wooden skewers soaked in water for at least 2 hours

Kosher salt and freshly ground white pepper to taste

½ cup (125 mL) 35% whipping cream

½ cup (125 mL) fish stock

1 tsp (5 mL) granulated sugar

½ tsp (2 mL) wasabi powder

2 Tbsp (30 mL) unsalted butter, softened

THE RAINFORD METHOD

1. Fire up your charcoal or preheat your gas grill. You need a medium-high grilling temp of around 350°F (180°C). Prep the grill for cooking over direct heat.

2. Place a 24- x 4-inch (60 x 10 cm) sheet of aluminum foil over the grate.

3. Meanwhile, combine the grapeseed oil, sesame oil and bay leaves in a resealable plastic bag. Add the tuna and marinate for at least 20 minutes at room temperature or in the fridge for up to 2 hours.

4. Remove the tuna from the marinade and thread each piece onto a skewer to resemble a lollipop. Season with salt and pepper to taste.

5. Place the tuna on the grill. Cook for 30 seconds to 1 minute per side (medium-rare is the best way to serve this tuna).

6. Combine the whipping cream, fish stock, sugar and wasabi powder in a small saucepan. Bring to a boil. Season with salt to taste. Whisk in the butter until melted and combined. Use a hand blender to foam the cream mixture.

7. Arrange the tuna lollipops on a serving platter. Spoon the foam over the top.

Makes 8 servings

 Tip: *For the fluffiest foam, lift the hand blender up and down in the saucepan as you blend.*

FOIE GRAS with DRIED CRANBERRY and SHALLOT COMPOTE

Foie gras on the grill. If I need to say anything else then you're not getting it. And I mean really not getting it, because it will all be in my belly. It's a simple fact that I love foie gras almost as much as I love my wife.

½ cup (125 mL) dried cranberries
½ cup (125 mL) thinly sliced shallots
¼ cup (60 mL) port
¼ cup (60 mL) red wine vinegar
¼ cup (60 mL) simple syrup *(see opposite)*
Canola oil for greasing
1 piece Grade A foie gras (about 1 lb/500 g),
    chilled
Kosher salt and freshly cracked black
    pepper to taste
Sliced brioche
Olive oil for brushing

THE RAINFORD METHOD

1. Place the dried cranberries, shallots, port, red wine vinegar and simple syrup in a small saucepan. Bring to a boil, then reduce the heat to a simmer.

2. Simmer the cranberry mixture until it has reduced and the liquid is thick enough to coat the back of a spoon. Let cool completely.

3. Fire up your charcoal grill or preheat your gas grill. You need a medium-high temperature of around 350°F (180°C). Prep the grill for cooking over direct heat.

4. Lightly oil a large cast iron skillet. Place the skillet on the grill to heat.

5. Cut the foie gras into 1-inch (2.5 cm) slices, using a sharp knife dipped in ice-cold water and wiped dry between each slice. Season the foie gras with salt and pepper to taste.

6. Place the foie gras slices in a single layer in the hot skillet. Cook for 3 to 5 minutes on each side or until a meat thermometer registers an internal temperature of 140°F (60°C).

7. Brush the brioche slices with a little olive oil and toast them directly on the grill until golden on both sides. Top the brioche slices with the foie gras and drizzle with some cranberry and shallot compote.

Makes 8 servings

Simple Syrup
½ cup (125 mL) granulated sugar
½ cup (125 mL) water

THE RAINFORD METHOD

1. Stir together the sugar and water in a small saucepan. Bring to a boil over medium heat, stirring to dissolve the sugar. Simmer for 3 minutes, then remove from the heat.

Makes about ⅔ cups (160 mL)

 Tip: *It's easier to slice foie gras if both the knife and the foie gras are very cold.*

BEER and JUNiPER BERRY SALMON on a CEDAR PLANK

Here I've added a twist to an old favorite of mine. Cedar-planked salmon has been on my menu for years but in this version I added some beer to change up the flavor profile. Don't be afraid to try new things with old recipes. You never know what can happen.

½ cup (125 mL) olive oil

¼ cup (60 mL) lager (I use Stella Artois)

2 Tbsp (30 mL) juniper berries

1 lemon, zested

1 jalapeño chili

8 skin-on salmon fillets, each about 8 oz (250 g)

4 untreated cedar planks, soaked in cold water for at least 2 hours

½ tsp (2 mL) kosher salt

½ tsp (2 mL) freshly cracked black pepper

THE RAINFORD METHOD

1. Whisk together the olive oil, beer, juniper berries, lemon zest and jalapeño. Place in a resealable plastic bag with the salmon. Marinate for 30 minutes maximum.
2. Fire up your charcoal or preheat your gas grill. You need a medium grilling temp of around 325°F (160°C). Prep the grill for cooking over direct heat.
3. Place the cedar planks on the grill until they're dry and starting to crackle.
4. Remove the salmon from the marinade and season with the salt and pepper. Place the salmon on the planks. Cook, covered, for 15 to 20 minutes or until the fish flakes easily. Let the salmon stand for 3 to 5 minutes before serving.

Makes 8 servings

CRAB-FiLLED POTATO BOATS

The filling for these potato boats is topped with Japanese panko breadcrumbs which are a little coarser than regular breadcrumbs. This recipe makes 16 potato halves which seems like a lot until you have one . . . which leads to another.

2 lb (1 kg) canned crabmeat

8 medium russet potatoes, scrubbed

Olive oil for rubbing

Kosher salt to taste

¼ cup (60 mL) unsalted butter

1 white onion, finely diced

1 sweet red pepper, seeded and finely diced

8 egg yolks

½ bunch green onions
(green part only), thinly sliced

3 Tbsp (45 mL) finely chopped garlic

2 Tbsp (30 mL) mayonnaise

2 Tbsp (30 mL) fresh lemon juice

1 Tbsp (15 mL) Worcestershire sauce

1 ½ tsp (7.5 mL) hot sauce

½ tsp (2 mL) cayenne

Freshly ground black pepper to taste

2 cups (500 mL) panko breadcrumbs

THE RAINFORD METHOD

1. Drain the crabmeat through a fine-mesh strainer. Set aside.

2. Fire up your charcoal or preheat your gas grill. You need a medium grilling temp of around 325°F (160°C). Prep the grill for cooking over direct heat.

3. Prick the potatoes with a fork several times. Rub the potatoes with olive oil and season with salt to taste. Place the potatoes on the grill. Cook, turning occasionally, for about 1 hour or until tender and the skin is puffed up, golden brown and crispy. Let cool completely.

4. Meanwhile, melt the butter in a large skillet set over medium heat. Add the white onion and red pepper. Cook until tender but not browned. Set aside to cool.

5. Cut the potatoes in half and scoop out the flesh into a bowl, leaving a ⅛ inch (3 mm) rim around the edge. Reserve skins.

6. Mash the potato flesh until smooth and completely cooled. Stir in the reserved onion mixture, crab, egg yolks, green onions, garlic, mayonnaise, lemon juice, Worcestershire sauce, hot sauce, cayenne, and black pepper to taste until well combined.

7. Divide the crab filling among the reserved potato skins. Sprinkle with breadcrumbs and black pepper. Return the stuffed potatoes to the upper rack of the grill. Bake, covered, for 15 minutes or until heated through.

Makes 8 servings

Tip: *If you prefer, discard the potato skins and use the filling to make crab cakes: form the mixture into balls and coat in the panko breadcrumbs. Place on a soaked untreated maple plank on the grill and cook until heated through and crispy.*

CAST IRON SKILLET BISCUITS

When you have a hot fire and you're looking for more things to cook on it, add this biscuit recipe to your repertoire. I love putting the cast iron skillet on the grill and coming back about half an hour later to a taste of heaven.

2 ½ cups (625 mL) all-purpose flour, sifted
½ cup (125 mL) cold unsalted butter, cut into small cubes
⅓ cup (80 mL) shredded aged white cheddar
1 Tbsp (15 mL) granulated sugar
2 ½ tsp (12 mL) baking powder
½ tsp (2 mL) kosher salt
¾ cup (185 mL) buttermilk
1 egg
Canola oil for greasing

THE RAINFORD METHOD

1. Fire up your charcoal grill and prep the grill for cooking over indirect heat by placing 10 to 12 lump charcoal briquettes directly under where the cast iron skillet will go and placing the remaining coals on the other side of the grill. You need a medium-high temperature of around 350°F (180°C). For gas grills, preheat the grill to medium-high then turn off one burner to achieve indirect heat.
2. Combine the flour, butter, cheddar, sugar, baking powder and salt in a large bowl. Mix by hand until the mixture resembles coarse crumbs.
3. Add the buttermilk and egg. Mix until the dough is moist and sticky.
4. Turn the dough out onto a lightly floured work surface and knead gently until smooth. Roll the dough out to 1 inch (2.5 cm) thickness and cut into eight even-size portions. Form into rounds.
5. Grease a 12-inch (30 cm) cast iron skillet with the oil. Arrange the dough rounds in the skillet. Place the skillet on the grill. Bake, covered as much as possible, for 30 to 40 minutes or until a toothpick inserted in the center of the biscuits comes out clean. Let cool on a wire rack.

Makes 8 biscuits

Tip: *Baking is something that can be done outside as well as inside. Treat your barbecue like an oven and keep the lid closed. This biscuit recipe is a winner but don't limit yourself to biscuits; try cakes, pies and anything else you can think of to bake.*

WHEN I SIT DOWN TO WRITE RECIPES the process can be lengthy. The first version is improvised and, from there, I create a framework so it will work for you. I like to write recipes as if I'm your older brother who's made a few trips around the culinary block, and share with you as much information as I can.

This menu finishes off my fish and shellfish section and although I've included another salmon recipe (after all, you can't have too many!), I've also added lobster finished with a little tarragon butter, and a stuffed jumbo shrimp appetizer (probably my favorite way to do them).

FINDING NEW FLAVORS FOR FISH

Bacon-Wrapped **JUMBO SHRIMP** *Stuffed with Crab*

GRILLED LOBSTER TAILS *with Truffle-Tarragon Butter*

Planked **JERK-STYLE WILD SALMON**

ARCTIC CHAR, SHRIMP AND MUSSELS *in Foil*

Grilled **GREEN TOMATOES**

BACON-WRAPPED JUMBO SHRIMP STUFFED WITH CRAB

Shrimp

8 jumbo shrimp (8/10 count),
    peeled and deveined with tail left intact
8 oz (250 g) canned crabmeat
½ white onion, finely diced
½ sweet red pepper, seeded and finely diced
½ bunch green onions (green parts only),
    thinly sliced
4 tsp (20 mL) panko breadcrumbs
2 tsp (10 mL) mayonnaise
2 tsp (10 mL) fresh lemon juice
1 tsp (5 mL) Worcestershire sauce

½ tsp (2 mL) finely chopped garlic
½ tsp (2 mL) hot sauce
Kosher salt and freshly ground
    black pepper to taste
8 slices bacon
1 untreated cedar plank,
    soaked in water for at least 2 hours

Dark Rum Glaze

½ cup (125 mL) dark rum
½ cup (125 mL) apple juice
¼ cup (60 mL) fresh lemon juice

THE RAINFORD METHOD

1. With a small, sharp knife, make an incision in the back of each shrimp, being careful not to cut all the way through. Open each shrimp like a book.

2. For the stuffing, mix together the crab, white onion, red pepper, green onions, breadcrumbs, mayonnaise, lemon juice, Worcestershire sauce, garlic, hot sauce, and salt and pepper to taste in a bowl.

3. Spoon crab mixture into the incision in each shrimp, being careful not to overfill them.

4. Roll each shrimp in a slice of bacon to form a cylinder shape (see Tip), then chill in the refrigerator for at least 1 hour or until firm.

5. Fire up your charcoal or preheat your gas grill. You need a medium-high grilling temp of around 350°F (180°C). Prep the grill for cooking over direct heat.

6. To make the glaze, place the rum, apple juice and lemon juice in a small saucepan and simmer over medium heat for 15 to 20 minutes or until the mixture has reduced and reaches a glaze consistency.

7. Place the cedar plank on the grill until it starts to crackle. This will take 10 to 12 minutes.

8. Place the shrimp on the cedar plank. Cook for 10 to 12 minutes or until the bacon is crisp. Brush with the dark rum glaze for the last 3 minutes of cooking.

Makes 8 servings

Tip: *Use plastic wrap to help shape the shrimp once you have rolled them in the bacon.*

GRiLLED LOBSTER TAiLS
with TRUFFLE-TARRAGON BUTTER

Lobster is one thing that most people can't get enough of. Although fresh is always best, this recipe also works well with frozen lobster tails.

8 shell-on lobster tails, each 8 to 10 oz (250 to 300 g)
1 cup (250 mL) olive oil
1 lemon, zested and juiced
1 Tbsp (15 mL) paprika
1 tsp (5 mL) freshly ground white pepper
1 tsp (5 mL) garlic powder
Truffle-Tarragon Butter (*recipe follows*)
Lemon wedges to serve

THE RAINFORD METHOD

1. Cut down the center of the underside of the lobster tails with a sharp knife. Cut all the way through but leave the end of the tail attached. Loosen the meat from the shells but don't remove the shells.
2. Whisk together the olive oil, lemon zest and juice, paprika, pepper and garlic powder in a shallow dish. Add the lobster tails, turning to coat with the marinade. Marinate in the refrigerator for 2 hours.
3. Fire up your charcoal or preheat your gas grill. You need a medium-high grilling temp of around 350°F (180°C). Prep the grill for cooking over direct heat.
4. Remove the lobster tails from the marinade and place on the grill, meat-side down. Cook for 4 minutes. Give the lobster tails a quarter turn (to give cross-wise grill marks) and continue cooking for another 4 minutes. Flip the lobster tails and cook on the shell side for 3 to 5 minutes or until the lobster tails are opaque and firm to the touch.
5. Top the hot lobster tails with slices of truffle-tarragon butter (*see recipe on following page*), letting the butter melt into the lobster meat. Serve with lemon wedges.

▶

Makes 8 servings

TRUFFLE-TARRAGON BUTTER

½ cup (125 mL) unsalted butter, softened
1 Tbsp (15 mL) finely chopped fresh tarragon
1 Tbsp (15 mL) finely chopped fresh parsley
1 tsp (5 mL) finely grated lemon zest
½ tsp (2 mL) white truffle oil
Kosher salt to taste

THE RAINFORD METHOD

1. Place the butter, tarragon, parsley, lemon zest, truffle oil and salt to taste in a bowl. Using a rubber spatula, beat well until fully incorporated.
2. Transfer the butter to a large piece of wax paper and shape into a log. Wrap tightly and chill until firm.

Makes about ½ cup (125 mL)

PLANKED JERK-STYLE WiLD SALMON

I can never forget my roots on the island of Jamaica, and I have to give my mom and dad all the credit for this recipe. Their love is what makes me want to keep celebrating these childhood memories—and recipes.

8 wild salmon steaks, each about 8 oz (250 g)
4 Tbsp (60 mL) Jerk Marinade *(see Rainford's Staple Recipes, page xvii)*
4 untreated cedar planks, soaked in water for at least 2 hours

THE RAINFORD METHOD

1. Carefully remove the backbone from each salmon steak, then gently remove the pin bones. Make sure to feel the salmon for bones by running your fingers over both sides.
2. Once the bones have been removed, cut about 2 inches (5 cm) of skin away from the flesh on one side of each salmon steak, leaving the skin attached. Tuck the ends of each salmon steak in and wrap the flap of skin round them to make perfectly circular steaks.
3. Take eight 8-inch (20 cm) pieces of butcher's twine and tie one round each salmon steak to secure it, just like you would put a belt on.
4. Spread the jerk marinade all over the salmon steaks. Marinate for at least 20 minutes at room temperature or up to 2 hours in the fridge.
5. Fire up your charcoal or preheat your gas grill. You need a medium-high grilling temp of around 350°F (180°C). Prep the grill for cooking over direct heat.
6. Place the cedar planks on the grill until the planks become dry and start to crackle. Place the salmon steaks on the planks. Reduce the heat to medium-low, 300°F (150°C).
7. Cook, covered, for 15 to 20 minutes or until salmon flakes easily when tested with a fork. Serve with a few traditional Jamaican Snacks *(see Tip)*.

Makes 8 servings

Tip: *To make Jamaican Snacks, cut 1 loaf Jamaican hard dough bread into ½-inch (1 cm) slices. Brush each slice with a little olive oil and lightly toast on the grill for barbecue flavor. Serve with Kola Champagne (soda pop from the islands).*

ARCTIC CHAR, SHRiMP and MUSSELS in Foil

This recipe can be prepared hours before your buddies come over, making it a terrific entertaining dish.

16 pieces aluminum foil, each 12 inches (30 cm) long
2 sweet yellow peppers, seeded and julienned
6 plum tomatoes, cored, seeded and julienned
2 leeks (white part only), washed and julienned
2 small carrots, julienned
1 fennel bulb, julienned
8 cloves garlic, very thinly sliced
4 lemons, 2 very thinly sliced and 2 juiced
4 lb (1.8 kg) arctic char fillet, cut into 8 pieces
32 medium shrimp (16/20 count), in their shells
2 lb (1 kg) mussels, scrubbed and de-bearded
½ cup (125 mL) dry white wine, such as a Chardonnay
4 Tbsp (60 mL) dry vermouth
1 cup (250 mL) cold unsalted butter, cubed
½ cup (125 mL) very thinly sliced fresh basil
Kosher salt and freshly ground black pepper to taste

THE RAINFORD METHOD

1. Fire up your charcoal or preheat your gas grill. You need a medium grilling temp of around 325°F (160°C). Prep the grill for cooking over direct heat.
2. Stack the pieces of foil in pairs, then lay them out on a work surface, assembly-line fashion, to make 8 double-layer pieces of foil.
3. Divide the yellow peppers, tomatoes, leeks, carrots, fennel, garlic and sliced lemons evenly among the 8 pieces of foil.
4. Top each portion of vegetables with 1 piece of arctic char, 4 shrimp and an equal amount of mussels.
5. Whisk together the lemon juice, white wine and vermouth. Spoon the lemon mixture evenly over the seafood.
6. Top each portion with an equal amount of butter and basil. Season with salt and pepper to taste.
7. Fold the foil over the ingredients to enclose them (like a panzarotti) and crimp the edges tightly to make sure the steam can't get out.
8. Place the pouches on the grill. Cook for 25 minutes, then check one pouch carefully, avoiding the steam that escapes, to check the fish and seafood are cooked. Serve in the aluminum foil pouches.

Makes 8 servings

GRiLLED GREEN TOMATOES

We've all heard of fried green tomatoes so naturally I wanted to see if they could be done on the grill. Boy, can they ever! Simple flavors always work well on the barbecue.

½ tsp (2 mL) granulated sugar
4 large green heirloom tomatoes, halved (if green tomatoes are not available, you can use red)
Olive oil for greasing
1 cup (250 mL) dry breadcrumbs
3 Tbsp (45 mL) butter, melted
3 Tbsp (45 mL) pale ale (I use Alexander Keith's India Pale Ale)
½ tsp (2 mL) dried oregano leaves
½ tsp (2 mL) dried basil leaves
½ tsp (2 mL) dried marjoram leaves
Kosher salt and freshly ground black pepper to taste

THE RAINFORD METHOD

1. Fire up your charcoal or preheat your gas grill. You need a medium grilling temp of around 325°F (160°C). Prep the grill for cooking over direct heat.
2. Sprinkle the sugar over the cut side of each tomato. Arrange tomatoes, cut-sides up, on a lightly oiled baking sheet or tin foil.
3. Toss together the breadcrumbs, butter, beer, oregano, basil, marjoram, and salt and pepper to taste. Top each tomato with 2 Tbsp (30 mL) of the breadcrumb mixture.
4. Place baking sheet directly on the grill. Cook, covered, for 20 to 30 minutes or until warmed through.

Makes 8 servings

I HAVE A REALLY GOOD FRIEND called Richard Cazeau who hosts a television show in Canada. When we hang out I always ask him what kind of food he likes to eat. Needless to say, one of our discussions spawned this menu. He doesn't know it yet but I've included a slaw recipe that's a shout-out to his Haitian background.

This is the last menu and, I have to say, was the most fun to create and eat. From the quick and delicious sliders to the grilled pizza, everything can be done in advance so you can hang out with your guests. How cool is that?!

Throughout this book I hope I've been able to help make you a better cook, because a happy chef makes a happy kitchen and happy meals.

20

BARBECUING— JUST BECAUSE YOU CAN

Grilled **MARGARITA PIZZA**

Ground **LAMB SLIDERS** with Tzatziki

Grilled **CORN ON THE COB** with Maple-Bourbon Butter

RICHARD CAZ'S HAITIAN SLAW

Spicy **CORNBREAD MUFFINS**

GRiLLED MARGARiTA PiZZA

Grilled pizza is something I've been playing with for years. My wife and daughters once tried a grilled pizza at one of the large chain restaurants and were very disappointed. So what do you do when you get let down? You develop your own recipe and use flavors you know will work. This is an easy, tasty recipe that you must try at your next dinner party.

Dough
1 cup (250 mL) warm water
1 package dry active yeast
1 tsp (5 mL) liquid honey
2 cups (500 mL) all-purpose flour (approx.)
1 tsp (5 mL) kosher salt
¼ cup (60 mL) extra virgin olive oil (approx.)

Balsamic Reduction
2 cups (500 mL) balsamic vinegar

Pizza Sauce
2 cups (500 mL) drained, canned
      San Marzano-style whole tomatoes
3 Tbsp (45 mL) extra virgin olive oil
2 Tbsp (30 mL) freshly grated Parmesan cheese
2 garlic cloves coarsely chopped
2 tsp (10 mL) dried oregano leaves
1 tsp (5 mL) granulated sugar
½ tsp (2 mL) kosher salt
½ tsp (2 mL) ground black pepper

Toppings
1 large fresh mozzarella ball, thinly sliced
20 fresh basil leaves
Extra virgin olive oil for drizzling

THE RAINFORD METHOD

1. For the dough, stir together the water and yeast until the yeast has dissolved. Stir in the honey. Let stand for 5 minutes or until frothy.
2. Stir together the flour and salt in a separate bowl. Make a well the center and add the yeast mixture and ¼ cup (60 mL) oil. Stir with your fingers, gradually incorporating the dry ingredients, until the dough forms a ball. (If the dough seems too sticky, add a bit more flour.)
3. Transfer the dough to a lightly floured surface. Knead gently for 5 minutes or until the dough is smooth and elastic (it will be slightly sticky).
4. Form the dough into a ball and place in a large, oiled bowl. Roll dough to lightly coat it in oil. Cover the bowl with plastic wrap and place in a warm spot for 1 hour or until the dough has doubled in size. Punch down the dough and form into 2 even-size balls.

▶

5. Meanwhile, make the balsamic reduction by placing the vinegar in a small saucepan set over medium heat. Simmer for 30 to 40 minutes or until the vinegar is thick enough to coat the back of a spoon and is very sweet. Remove from the heat and set aside.

6. For the pizza sauce, place the tomatoes, olive oil, Parmesan, garlic, oregano, sugar, salt and black pepper in a blender. Blend until smooth. Set aside.

7. Fire up your charcoal grill and prep the grill for cooking over indirect heat. You need a high temperature of around 400°F (200°C) to grill the pizzas. For gas grills, preheat the grill to high then turn off one burner to achieve indirect heat.

8. Roll out each piece of dough on a lightly floured surface to a 12-inch (30 cm) round. Grease the grate well and place the dough rounds directly on the grate over direct heat. Grill for 2 minutes or until well marked and slightly blistered. Turn the crusts over and cook for an additional 30 seconds or until very lightly charred.

9. Transfer the crusts from the grill to a clean work surface, darker-side up. Spread half of the pizza sauce evenly over each crust and top with mozzarella. Return the pizzas to the grill over indirect heat. Cook for 4 to 5 minutes or until the cheese has melted.

10. Just before serving, tear the basil leaves into pieces and scatter over each pizza. Drizzle each pizza with olive oil and some of the balsamic reduction.

Each pizza makes 8 appetizer servings

 Tip: *Grilling a pizza changes its flavor profile, adding great smoky notes. Don't worry if you don't have a pizza stone as the dough in this recipe is designed to go directly on the grill. Follow the steps and see what kind of magic you can create.*

GROUND LAMB SLiDERS with TZATZiKi

3 lb (1.5 kg) ground lamb
½ cup (125 mL) kalamata olives,
    pitted and coarsely chopped
¼ cup (60 mL) grated onion
4 cloves garlic, finely grated
1 jalapeño chili, seeded and diced
2 tsp (10 mL) ground cloves
2 tsp (10 mL) ground cumin
2 tsp (10 mL) freshly ground black pepper
Kosher salt to taste
1 red onion, cut in half and thinly sliced
2 Tbsp (30 mL) red wine vinegar
1 Tbsp (15 mL) granulated sugar
24 slider buns or small dinner rolls
Tzatziki *(see opposite)*

Tzatziki
1 cup (250 mL) peeled, seeded and
    coarsely grated English cucumber
2 cups (500 mL) Greek-style plain yogurt
¼ cup (60 mL) finely chopped
    fresh mint leaves
2 Tbsp (30 mL) fresh lemon juice
1 Tbsp (15 mL) olive oil
4 cloves garlic, finely grated
Kosher salt and freshly ground
    black pepper to taste

THE RAINFORD METHOD

1. Mix together the ground lamb, olives, grated onion, garlic, jalapeño, cloves, cumin, pepper and salt to taste until well combined.
2. Divide the mixture into 24 equal portions and form into patties. Refrigerate until firm.
3. Meanwhile, toss red onion with vinegar and sugar in a bowl. Marinate for at least 1 hour at room temperature.
4. Fire up your charcoal or preheat your gas grill. You need a medium-high grilling temp of around 350°F (180°C). Prep the grill for cooking over direct heat.
5. Place the patties on the grill. Cook for 3 to 4 minutes per side or until cooked through. Just before the patties are ready, toast the buns until golden. Serve the patties on buns, topped with tzatziki and the marinated onions.

Makes 8 servings

THE RAINFORD METHOD

1. Squeeze the cucumber firmly to remove any excess liquid.
2. Stir together the cucumber, yogurt, mint, lemon juice, olive oil, garlic, and salt and pepper to taste in a serving bowl. Refrigerate until ready to serve.

Makes about 3 cups (750 mL)

Tip: *Before forming the meat mixture into patties, make a tiny patty and grill it up to ensure its flavor and seasoning are to your taste.*

GRiLLED CORN ON THE COB
with MAPLE-BOURBON BUTTER

The fresher the corn, the better it tastes, and there's nothing finer than picking your own corn and being able to grill it straightaway.

½ cup (125 mL) finely chopped fresh chives

½ cup (125 mL) unsalted butter, softened

1 Tbsp (15 mL) pure maple syrup

1 tsp (5 mL) bourbon

Kosher salt to taste

8 ears peaches-and-cream corn, in the husk

THE RAINFORD METHOD

1. Place the chives, butter, maple syrup, bourbon, and salt to taste in a bowl. Using a rubber spatula, beat the mixture well until fully incorporated.
2. Transfer the butter to large piece of wax paper and shape into a log. Wrap tightly and refrigerate until firm.
3. Fire up your charcoal or preheat your gas grill. You need a medium-high grilling temp of around 350°F (180°C). Prep the grill for cooking over direct heat.
4. Remove the tough outer layers of husk from the corn, leaving the thin, tender layers intact.
5. Place the corn on the grill, leaving space between each ear. Cook, turning every 2 minutes, for 8 to 10 minutes or until the husks are completely charred.
6. Remove the corn from the grill. Carefully peel back the husks and serve with the maple-bourbon butter.

Makes 8 servings

 Tip: *You can also soak the corn in water before grilling but it will steam the corn and reduce the smoky flavor that I love so much.*

RICHARD CAZ'S HAITIAN SLAW

Feel free to kick the heat up on this—the hotter the better!

4 cups (1 L) shredded savoy cabbage
¼ cup (60 mL) julienned carrot
¼ cup (60 mL) seeded and julienned sweet yellow pepper
¼ cup (60 mL) mayonnaise
¼ cup (60 mL) sour cream
1 Tbsp (15 mL) cider vinegar
½ tsp (2 mL) Jerk Marinade *(see Rainford's Staple Recipes, page xvii)*
½ tsp (2 mL) hot sauce
Kosher salt and freshly ground black pepper to taste

THE RAINFORD METHOD

1. Toss together the cabbage, carrot and yellow pepper in a serving bowl.
2. Stir together the mayonnaise, sour cream, cider vinegar, jerk marinade and hot sauce until well combined.
3. Pour the dressing over the cabbage mixture and toss well. Season with salt and pepper to taste and toss again.

Makes 8 to 10 servings

 **Tip:** *To speed up prep time, shred the cabbage and carrots using a box grater, or a mandoline slicer with the julienne blade fitted.*

SPiCY CORNBREAD MUFFiNS

For those who like to kick the heat up, this one's for you. The recipe works with or without the jalapeños but don't be afraid to add them. Spicy is good!

Softened unsalted butter or nonstick baking spray for greasing
2 cups (500 mL) all-purpose flour, sifted
¾ cup (185 mL) extra-fine cornmeal
3 Tbsp (45 mL) baking powder
1 tsp (5 mL) kosher salt
1 egg
⅔ cup (160 mL) buttermilk
⅓ cup (80 mL) unsalted butter, melted
1 cup (250 mL) shredded aged white cheddar
4 jalapeño chilies, seeded and finely diced

THE RAINFORD METHOD

1. Fire up your charcoal grill and prep the grill for cooking over indirect heat. You need a low temperature of around 300°F (150°C) maximum. For gas grills, preheat the grill to low then turn off one burner to achieve indirect heat.
2. Grease a 12-cup muffin pan with butter or nonstick baking spray. Set aside.
3. Stir together the flour, cornmeal, baking powder and salt in a large bowl.
4. In a separate bowl, whisk together the egg, buttermilk and melted butter.
5. Using a wooden spoon, stir the wet ingredients into the dry until well combined. Stir in the cheese and jalapeños. Divide the batter evenly among the prepared muffin cups.
6. Place the muffin pan on the grill over indirect heat. Cook, covered, for 30 to 40 minutes or until a toothpick comes out clean when inserted in the center of a muffin. Let the muffins cool in the pan on a wire rack for 5 to 10 minutes before removing them from the pan. Serve warm.

Makes 12 muffins

iNDEX

ACKNOWLEDGMENTS

I'D FIRST LIKE TO SAY THANK YOU so much to my wonderful team for all your hard work on this project. A book like this doesn't come together overnight and it takes a lot of people to get to this point. We sure had a blast making this book and I hope my fans have just as much fun reading and creating as we did!

Eb Reinbergs, my friend and lawyer, who has helped me navigate the waters for years, is a person who deserves congratulations. When the people you trust support what you're doing it just makes life that much easier.

Thanks, too, to Greg Cosway, my manager, who saw something in me and has worked tirelessly to bring my dreams to fruition. I'm blessed to part of the Chef Events Canada team (chefevents.ca) and the future looks bright and filled with delicious opportunities!

I thank Les Murray, a key member of my management team, for his adept ear and kind soul.

And, Ted Reader—Teddy, thanks, man. You are truly a master of barbecue and I love that we can grill and smoke together. Life just doesn't get any better than that!

Mike and Mia who worked tirelessly on the photography for this book to make it look and feel first class, your hard work did not go unnoticed and your talent is second to none! I look forward to working with you on future projects. You have a great family and I know you've made your girls proud.

Chef Michael Pasto who happens to be one of the top chefs in the country took time out of his busy schedule to work by my side until the job was done right. Michael, you are an invaluable resource and all your hard work can be seen and enjoyed in this book now and forever! I sincerely hope that I will be able to return the favor one day.

Leavoy Rowe Beef Co., Rod Rowe, your meat is world class! It's been great having you on board for this book and it has been a pleasure grilling with your products. Dinner is on me any time you like; you guys just have to bring the steaks!

To Duff Dixon of Ontario Gas BBQ—who runs the world's largest barbecue store and has a heart to match!—thanks for all of your support. You certainly had a big hand in making this book tasty and delicious, my friend! Barbecue fans and grill meisters, you have to visit this store or, as I like to call it, "the shrine"! Check out bbqs.com and set your world on fire.

Leslie Gadoury and my good friends at Ravenswood, we certainly enjoyed your products while making this book. Oh, and we enjoyed cooking with them as well! Keep making great wines and we will keep enjoying them. Thank you, thank you!

Charlie Angelakos and my numerous friends at Labatt, what can I tell you? A hot grill and cold, delicious beer is a magical combination! Thanks guys for cooling us off with tasty brews. We loved grilling with these products and I know my fans will enjoy grilling up the recipes as much as we did creating them!

Napoleon Gourmet Grills are hot, sexy grills! I love these grills! Wolfgang, Ingrid, Stephen and Chris (the Schroeter family) and David Coulson and team, thanks so much for manufacturing and marketing grills of the highest quality and especially for believing in the Rainford team!

Caiti McLelland, who deals with this temperamental chef with kid gloves but still finds a way to get everything done on time, a huge thank you to you.

Thanks to Marian Staresinic, a new team member at Chef Events Canada who has added her expertise as a chef, food writer and marketing manager to the mix.

Nola Woodall, thanks for that second set of eyes a book like this needs.

Robert McCullough and his team at Random House of Canada, thanks so much.

My family, James W. Robinson III and his family, Uncle Horace, Aunt Norma Jones, Uncle Denis and Aunt Barbra, Uncle Timothy Jones, Uncle Paul and Aunt Eunell Jones, Aunt Cherry, Aunt Winnie (the Jones side of my family). Joseph Palumbo, Maria and Mario Palumbo.

Also Nevin Blair, Richard Zephyrine, Kevin Brauch, Brad and Caroline Rohrig, Jakob Hausmann, Donovan Dill, Candida Ness, Paula Davies, Mark Strong, Lyriq Bent, Damon Allen, Michael "Pinball" Clemons, Edward Hollaway, Brian Morris, Peter Warren, Matt West, Eldy Gouthro, George Sully, Iulia Dragut, Cliff Klein, Radu Zarnescy, Dan Chişu, Marlon Durrant, Joe Baker and Colin Tobias.

Lastly, thanks to my mom, Enis Rainford; my dad, Alvin Rainford; Richard Rainford and his family; Howard Rainford and his family; Marcia Rainford and her family, and Alvin Jr. Rainford.